COLLABORATIVE DISCIPLINE

for At-Risk Students

A Complete Step-by-Step
Activities Program for Grades 7-12

George H. Byers, Ph.D.

**THE CENTER FOR APPLIED
RESEARCH IN EDUCATION**
West Nyack, New York 10994

Prentice-Hall International (UK) Limited, *London*
Prentice-Hall of Australia Pty. Limited, *Sydney*
Prentice-Hall Canada, Inc., *Toronto*
Prentice-Hall Hispanoamericana, S.A., *Mexico*
Prentice-Hall of India Private Limited, *New Delhi*
Prentice-Hall of Japan, Inc., *Tokyo*
Simon & Schuster Asia Pte. Ltd., *Singapore*
Editora Prentice-Hall do Brasil, Ltda., *Rio de Janeiro*

©1994 *by*
PRENTICE HALL

10   9   8   7   6   5   4   3   2

Library of Congress Cataloging-in Publication Data

Byers, George H.
    Collaborative discipline for at-risk students : a peer support activities
program for grades 7–12 / George H. Byers.
        p.   cm.
    Includes index.
    ISBN 0-87628-122-6
    1. Peer counseling of students—United States. 2. School discipline—
United States. 3. Behavior modification—United States.
I. Title.
LB1027.5.B89   1994   94-23390
371.4'04—dc20   CIP

ISBN 0-87628-122-6

**THE CENTER FOR APPLIED RESEARCH
IN EDUCATION**
West Nyack, NY 10994
A Simon & Schuster Company

On the World Wide Web at http://www.phdirect.com

Printed in the United States of America

This activities guide is dedicated to the Central Independent High School staff of the Alternative Schools Department, Santa Clara County Office of Education, San Jose, California. It was a privilege to be a co-worker with such competent and caring professionals.

Acknowledgments

I would like to express my gratitude and appreciation to the multitude of knowledgeable educators that shared their expertise with me. John Malloy and the Foundry school staff were especially helpful in this process. This sharing of successful ideas, techniques, and methods have helped to formulate this activities guide.

I would also like to acknowledge Susan Kolwicz, Eve Mossman, and Emily Adler for their tireless efforts in the editing, revisions, rewriting, and formatting of the original manuscript. Their outstanding ideas and directions made it possible to formulate this guide.

About the Author

George H. Byers (Ph.D. in Guidance/Counseling, Columbia Pacific University) has combined 18 years as a teacher at the middle and high school levels with 16 years as a teacher and counselor of at-risk students (in California) to gain a broad understanding of the educational needs of all students. He has designed and implemented a community school, independent study and career/work experience programs, a community network for youths, and Peer Support Teams, for at-risk students. Through utilizing Peer Support Teams as a vehicle to provide at-risk students with sound academic, vocational, communication, critical thinking, and interpersonal skills, 80% of these students remained in school for one year to meet their long-range educational goals. Dr. Byers works as a consultant in the field of Alternative Education.

About the Book

One of the most urgent problems facing teachers and counselors today is how to rescue at-risk students before they drop out of high school. To better understand the gravity of this problem, let's explore the question, "Why are at-risk students prone to fail in school?" Historically, many at-risk youths have not been properly loved or cared for, and they have been physically and verbally abused by family members. Consequently, they come to school with:

- low self-esteem and behavioral problems
- lack of trust and respect for others
- communication problems
- difficulty in working cooperatively with others

Accordingly, they tend to strike back at their classmates and teachers to:

- get attention for misbehaving
- gain power by challenging authority
- seek revenge by hurting others verbally or physically

As any educator can tell you, this negative behavior leads to disciplinary problems in the classroom. Therefore, teachers waste valuable time disciplining students instead of teaching. This negative classroom environment is detrimental to student success in school.

The purpose of this guide is to provide teachers, counselors, parents, and students with a collaborative process that diminishes disciplinary problems. Student support teams and the teacher and/or counselor facilitate this process through a sequence of bonding activities designed to teach at-risk students positive ways to behave in class. Teachers and counselors are given proven and practical how-to-do-it instructions to facilitate these activities.

DESCRIPTION OF DISCIPLINE PREVENTION PROGRAM

To establish a sound foundation for positive discipline in the classroom, the following components must complement the bonding activities:

- The teacher and counselor must gain an understanding of each student's behavioral problems.
- The teacher must establish ground rules for positive behavior during a class activity.
- The teacher must set consequences for misbehavior in class.
- The teacher must initiate intervention techniques to properly discipline at-risk students for misbehavior.

These components utilized together with the bonding activities comprise the Collaborative Discipline Prevention Program. Here students learn positive communication and problem-solving skills, and parents support the teacher and their child to enhance positive discipline in school and at home. To gain a clear idea of what will be covered in Sections 1–6, refer to the following overview.

OVERVIEW OF SECTIONS 1–6

Section 1—Bonding Activities

Because of the negative behavioral characteristics of at-risk students, bonding activities are designed to replace negativity with positive behavior. Through these bonding activities students learn to:

- connect with classmates and school staff in a friendly and positive way
- relate to and communicate with classmates and school staff through positive means
- build high self-esteem by being a capable and contributing student and teammate
- work cooperatively with others as a member of a student support team
- assume responsibility for their own behavior and the behavior of teammates
- exude positive peer influence to assist teammates to behave in class and excel in their studies
- provide positive support to teammates to enhance their self-esteem and confidence in reaching their educational goals

By learning and practicing this positive behavior, negative behavior diminishes and discipline problems are negligible.

Section 2—Communication Activities

At-risk students tend to alienate their classmates through poor communication skills. Often at-risk students use:

- verbal put-down statements
- name calling
- poor listening skills
- negative hand gestures and facial expressions

Negative peer pressure reinforces the need to exhibit this behavior in the classroom. Therefore, some at-risk students purposefully use this behavior to disturb classmates or hassle the teacher. This behavior causes conflict among students or between students and the teacher, and thus creates disciplinary problems for the teacher. To counter this misbehavior, teachers and counselors provide training and incentives for students to:

- replace verbal *"put-down"* statements with *"build-up"* statements
- start a conversation and be a good listener
- recognize and avoid poor listening habits
- listen from the heart and display empathy
- observe verbal and nonverbal communication patterns of others
- use positive *I-messages* to replace negative *"You"* statements
- use assertive behavior to resist negative peer pressure

Consequently, teachers have fewer disciplinary problems as students communicate well with classmates and school staff.

Section 3—Problem-Solving Activities

Typical at-risk students lack the ability to make good decisions or cope with personal problems. Because of this lack of good judgment and their vulnerability to "street" activity, at-risk youths are prone to get involved in nonproductive activities, such as:

Violence

—Major degree: gangs and criminal activities, shootings or carrying guns to school or in the community (It is estimated that 100,000 American students carry guns to school daily.)

—Minor degree: conflict between students (name calling, pushing, fighting) in school or in the community

ALCOHOL AND OTHER DRUG ABUSE

—Major degree: alcohol or other drug addiction

—Minor degree: partying on weekends, limited daily use

EARLY SEXUAL ACTIVITY

—Major degree: AIDS, venereal diseases, pregnancy and teenage parenting, abortion, babies born with addictions, prostitution

—Minor degree: petting, sex using contraceptive devices, sexual harassment

Participation in major degree activities usually leads to dropping out of school. Involvement in minor degree activities can lead to truancy problems. The residual effects from these activities can lead to peer and family problems, and behavior problems for at-risk youths. These problems can then lead to negative behavior in the classroom. To cope with or perhaps avoid these problems, students learn a **six-step critical thinking process** that teaches them how to:

1. Define and clarify a problem
2. Gather and review data
3. Analyze and evaluate data
4. Arrive at solutions and make decisions
5. Design and implement action plans
6. Review results of plans and make recommendations/revisions

Accordingly, at-risk students learn how to make good decisions and cope with personal problems. This training will carry over into the classroom. Consequently, students will sustain and flourish in class, and teachers will have fewer discipline problems.

Section 4—Career/Leisure Activities

This unit is designed to complement Section 3. Section 3 taught at-risk students how to say no to participation in violent, alcohol/drug, and sexual situations. Section 4 then gets at-risk students involved in productive career/leisure activities, diverting them from the nonproductive activities. Students learn how to:

- identify jobs and leisure activities that are compatible with their interests and abilities

- explore these jobs and leisure activities in order to select their top choices

- complete job and leisure action plans, and get started in their job and leisure activity selections

Consequently, students get involved in career exploration, work experience, and/or vocational training as well as leisure activities such as sports, music, drama, and arts and crafts. They have the opportunity to gain valuable skills and experiences in these activities.

Participation in these productive activities, instead of nonproductive activities, should enhance positive behavior in the classroom to complement the collaborative discipline process.

Section 5—Parenting Activities

Parents of at-risk students typically lack the necessary parenting skills to support their child. Some face the following obstacles:

—they are unable to conduct a meaningful conversation with their child

—they use put-down statements when correcting or disciplining their child

—they rarely attend parent meetings and lack interest in helping their child succeed in school.

This unit shows teachers and counselors how to motivate parents to attend school meetings and parenting classes. Through parenting classes parents learn how to:

- conduct meaningful conversations with their child

- use positive *I-messages* when disciplining their child

- enhance their child's self-esteem

- help their child cope with personal and family problems

Parents also get involved in the planning of their child's curriculum, long-range educational goals, and behavioral goals. Throughout this collaborative process, parents support the teacher and their child which helps diminish disciplinary problems in school and at home.

Section 6—Transitional Plans

Transitional plans are designed for students who have met their long-range educational goals. Student support team members help their teammates devise these plans. Without these plans and follow-up, at-risk students could "fall through the cracks." This unit provides teachers and counselors with the necessary know-how to:

- instruct student support team members in developing their transitional plans

- guide students in implementing their plans

- implement a follow-up plan to check student progress

- inform parents and get their support in the execution of their child's transitional plan

Because of this planning and support from students, teachers, counselors, and parents, at-risk students are given an excellent opportunity to continue their success in school.

Continuity in Completion of Educational Goals

At the beginning of the school year, the teacher, student, counselor, and parents will meet to arrive at and agree to the student's curriculum, long-range educational goals, and behavioral goals. When appropriate, they will agree on the student's job and leisure activity selections. During the remainder of the school year, students are supported by their teacher, counselor, parents, and student support team members to successfully:

- complete their long-range educational and behavioral goals
- participate in career and leisure interest activities

Students who have successfully met their goals will devise transitional plans, as described in Section 6.

Implementing Student Support Teams

In preparation for conducting activities as described in Sections 1–6, teachers and counselors must carefully review the guidelines for implementing student support team activities. These guidelines will provide teachers and counselors with the how-to-do-it instructions necessary to properly facilitate all activities. Refer to the next section, *Implementing Student Support Teams* immediately following this introduction.

Index

This guide provides an index that gives teachers and counselors immediate access to answers for solving discipline problems in the classroom. For example, if a teacher is having a problem with verbal abuse, the index will key the section and activities needed to curb this problem in the classroom. Refer to index for directions and useage.

George Byers

Introduction

IMPLEMENTING STUDENT SUPPORT TEAMS

Today's teachers and counselors have busy schedules and time restraints. Therefore, guidelines for conducting Student Support Team activities are designed for easy implementation. The following instructions provide a basis for implementing Student Support Teams. Leaders should carefully review these guidelines in preparation for leading activities.

Implementing Student Support Teams in the Classroom

Most at-risk students are not psychologically prepared to successfully begin a new school year. If there is no attempt to reverse their negative attitudes and behavior towards school, many of these students will fail, drop out, or never arrive in the first place. Accordingly, Section 1, Bonding Activities, should be used to prepare them for success in the instructional program.

A subject area teacher would begin the school year by conducting a bonding activity each class period. It would take eleven class periods to complete the bonding activities. A self-contained classroom teacher has the flexibility to spend the first two weeks of school conducting a variety of activities.

At-risk students usually become restless during a four- to five- period day within a self-contained classroom. To alleviate this restlessness, Community School programs in California interject a period of physical activity during the school day. Students generally play activities such as softball, volleyball, basketball, and so on. The teacher and/or counselor supervises these activities.

The suggested two-week schedule is an excellent plan to prepare at-risk students for the beginning of the school year.

Suggested Two-Week Schedule

Day 1 Orientation to the program
       Activity 1
       Academic assessment
       Physical Education and trust building activities

Day 2 Activity 2
       Learning style survey
       Career/leisure assessment
       Physical Education and trust building activities

Day 3 Activity 3
       Career/leisure assessment
       Physical Education and trust building activities
       Begin parent-student-teacher meetings

Day 4 Activity 4
       Physical Education and trust building activities
       Activity 5
       Continue parent-student-teacher meetings

Day 5 Field trip of choice
       Continue parent-student-teacher meetings

Day 6 Activity 6
       Physical Education and trust building activities
       Career/leisure exploration activities
       Continue parent-student-teacher meetings

Day 7 Activity 7
       Physical Education and trust building activities
       Career/leisure exploration
       Continue parent-student-teacher meetings

Day 8 Field trip of choice
       Continue parent-student-teacher meetings

Day 9 Activities 8 and 9
       Guest speaker
       Physical Education and trust building activities
       Career/leisure exploration activities
       Continue parent-student-teacher meetings

Day 10 Activities 10 and 11

> Physical Education and trust building activities
> Career/leisure exploration activities
> Continue parent-teacher-student meetings

In a subject area or self-contained classroom, student support teams would begin instruction through a cooperative learning process at the conclusion of the bonding activities. The teacher can then focus specifically on bonding activities or instruction to easily facilitate this dual responsibility. Teachers will use the provided index to select and conduct prescribed activities from Sections 1–6 as needed. Or, a counselor will coordinate with the teacher to conduct selected activities inside or outside of class.

An excellent approach is to conduct bonding activities through a summer program in preparation for school. Through this approach, student support teams would be ready to begin the school year without taking time away from the subject areas. Ideally, a teacher and a counselor would team up to cover the summer and regular school programs.

Another possibility would be to conduct an elective class for at-risk students. Students would attend class daily over an 18-week semester course. The course could be taught by a counselor who is assigned to work with at-risk students. Accordingly, he/she would coordinate with classroom teachers.

Suggested Semester Course

SECTION 1 ACTIVITIES:

> Week 1 Activities 1 to 5
> Week 2 Activities 6 to 10
> Week 3 Activity 11

SECTION 2 ACTIVITIES

> Week 3 Activities 1 to 3 and the Weekly Audit Review Meeting
> Week 4 Activities 4 to 7 and the Weekly Audit Review Meeting
> Week 5 Activities 8 to 10 and the Weekly Audit Review Meeting

SECTION 3 ACTIVITIES

> Week 5 Activity 1
> Week 6 Activities 2 to 5 and the Weekly Audit Review Meeting
> Week 7 Activities 6 to 9 and the Weekly Audit Review Meeting
> Week 8 Career/leisure assessment activities and the weekly review meeting
> Week 9 Career/leisure exploratory activities and the weekly review meeting

Week 10 Continue career/leisure exploratory activities and the weekly review meeting

Week 11 Designing and sharing of action plans to get team members involved in career/leisure activities; conduct weekly review meeting

Week 12 Activities 10 to 14 and weekly review meeting

Week 13 Activities 15 to 18 and weekly review meeting

Week 14 Implementation of the drug prevention community/school project; weekly review meeting

Week 15 Follow-up of Activity 14 and the review and revision of team members' action plan; pairing of student helpers to assist at-risk students in the implementation of revised action plans; conduct weekly review meeting

Week 16 Complete a cooperative learning research report on a key topic such as AIDS; conduct the weekly review meeting

Week 17 Continuation of the cooperative learning research report; conduct weekly review meeting

Week 18 Conclusion of the cooperative learning research report; conduct weekly review meeting

Conducting an Activity

In order for a leader to understand each part of an activity, the following format is used throughout the book:

- a stated *purpose* explaining the intention of an activity
- *performance skills* to be learned from an activity
- a list of *materials* needed to conduct an activity
- an *introduction* explaining the purpose and benefit of the activity
- an activity *procedure* listing the steps needed to conduct an activity
- a *discussion* period that helps students understand what they have learned
- an *appreciation* period that validates students for their positive contributions
- *instructional tips* needed to successfully conduct an activity
- an *anticipated results* section stating the expected outcome of an activity

Leading and Facilitating an Activity

To lead, monitor, and facilitate several teams simultaneously, the leader must adhere to specific guidelines, such as:

✓ Position yourself to see and work with all teams at the same time.

✓ Give teams simple and concise directions through a step-by-step approach.

✓ Act as a role model by demonstrating what you expect them to do.

✓ Stop an activity and review the ground rules during a poor team effort.

✓ Tell the students how much time will be allowed for each activity and monitor that time limit.

✓ Post the ground rules for conducting a team activity, explaining and reviewing these rules to student support teams as necessary.

✓ Move from team to team to observe and assist as needed

Check each team member's level of participation as follows:

✓ Are team members adhering to the ground rules for conducting an activity?

- be a good listener and don't interrupt or distract others
- show respect for others with no put-downs or arguments
- be an active participant and support your teammates
- observe confidentiality and don't gossip about others concerning personal matters

✓ Are a few people doing all of the talking or working with others or is there full participation?

✓ Are team members excited about the activity and having fun or are they lethargic, hostile, and so forth?

✓ Are team members working well on the task at hand, and who has assumed a leadership role?

The leader should carefully observe each team's focus on the ground rules for conducting an activity. Abiding by the ground rules will keep teams on task and eliminate negativity during an activity.

Facilitating Discussion and Brainstorming Activities

As activities become complex, students will be involved in discussion and brainstorming activities. When facilitating these activities, leaders should observe the following guidelines:

- Be sure that the teams have a clear understanding of the brainstorming topic.
  - Allow teams to arrive at their own brainstorming or discussion topics—ideas and discussion flow rapidly when the students are interested in the issue.
  - During a brainstorming or discussion period, each team member takes a turn and presents one thought at a time.

- Ask students to raise their hand to be recognized by the facilitator for participating during brainstorming and discussion sessions.
- Follow ground rules and show respect for others' ideas and opinions.
- Ask students to build on the ideas of others.
- If there is a lack of participation ask a strong participant a thought-provoking question—the participant's answer usually stimulates others to get involved in the discussion—and after an activity discuss the reasons for nonparticipation and arrive at ways to enhance student participation.

Forming Permanent Student Support Teams

Activities 1 to 7 are designed to enhance bonding among students and school staff, and to evaluate the cooperativeness of students during activities. To conduct these activities, students function as a class or on temporary teams—depending upon the nature of the activity. Students change teams from activity to activity to bond with all of their classmates, and the teacher observes how well various combinations of students work together. Students that bond well and work together effectively will make good permanent teammates. Other factors to consider when forming permanent teams are:

✓ placing proportionate numbers of active and inactive participants on separate teams

✓ observing how various combinations of students work cooperatively and rearranging students to form compatible teams

✓ placing students on teams with teammates they trust and respect

✓ dividing students that tend to get bored or easily distracted among the various teams

✓ dividing boys and girls proportionately among various teams

✓ dividing individuals proportionately in teams by race such as Black, Asian, Hispanic, and Caucasian

Students are placed on permanent teams during Activity 8. In Activities 8 to 11 they focus on how to function as a member of a support team. Supporting teammates to reach their educational goals binds them as teammates. They function as a team throughout the remainder of the activities in 2 to 6; and they assist each other in their studies via a cooperative learning process. Teams do not compete against each other.

Six students per team has been found to be an ideal number to work with in cooperative team activities. When working with at-risk students, a class of 18 to 24 students, or three to four teams is recommended. Refer to "Staffing" for variations in numbers of students.

Organizing Student Support Teams

When students function as student support teams in a classroom, they sit together in the same location around a table or in a cluster of desks arranged in a circle or a horseshoe alignment. Working together in close proximity enhances good teamwork and the facilitation of activities.

When working with a counseling group outside of class, the counselor must maintain cohesive coordination with the students' teachers. Good continuity between the counselor and the teachers is essential in transferring the following skills and behavioral practices:

✓ communication and critical thinking skills

✓ good work habits and attitudes

✓ positive behavioral practices (per behavioral code and contract)

The goal of this collaboration between the counselor and the teacher is to help at-risk students succeed in the classroom via this collaborative discipline process.

Staffing

A hard-core class of at-risk students should not go beyond 20 students per teacher and a teacher's aide because of the need for individualized instruction and the capability of managing these students in the classroom. To enhance a strong behavioral component, as described in this guide, a counselor should be on call to assist the teacher. With strong student support team leaders and an instructional aide, a Community School teacher was able to manage 28 typical at-risk students through this program.

Evaluation and Grading

The student support teams process is integrated into the instructional process of a self-contained or cooperative learning classroom, or in a counseling group; therefore, it is not necessary to arrive at a letter grade to evaluate a student's performance. However, the peer audit process evaluates a student's progress as a contributing member of his/her student support team. Refer to activity 11 in Section 1. Through the support that student team members provide each other, as described in Section 1, activities 8 to 11, they enhance the opportunity for each student to achieve a passing grade in a subject area class. Refer to activities 10 and 11 in Section 1.

Adapting Student Support Teams to Various School Settings

The possibilities for adapting the activities in this guide are numerous, and creative educators have the option to select activities to meet a special education need and design their own program or complement another educational program.

Accordingly, this guide can be used as a resource for educators to draw from throughout a school or school district. For example, an astute educator can adapt Student Support Teams for use in:

✓ a self-contained classroom in an alternative or special school setting

✓ a regular school classroom to complement a cooperative learning program

✓ a summer school program to complement a remedial or adventure program

✓ an elective class to complement a life skills curriculum

✓ a voluntary counseling group to help potential school drop outs to increase attendance and succeed in school

✓ a voluntary after-school program to help interested C or D letter grade students achieve B or A grades in school

✓ a prevention program in an inner-city school to replace gangs with Student Support Teams

✓ a juvenile institutional camp or ranch to enhance a student's successful transition back into the community

✓ and, specific units could be pulled out separately for the following reasons:

1. Section 1 can be used by a teacher to deter disciplinary problems and improve instruction via a collaborative discipline process.

2. The communication and critical thinking skills section can be used separately or in unison with a living skills class.

3. The career/leisure section can be used within a work experience or a career education program or class.

4. The parenting section can be used to start a parenting class or to use in conjunction with an existing curriculum.

5. The conflict resolution activities 7, 8, and 9 in Section 3 can be used to train conflict resolution mediators in a voluntary after-school program.

6. Sections 2 and 3 on communication and critical thinking skills can be used to train peer helpers or mentors in a voluntary after-school program.

Note: Refer to References and Resources sections to obtain contacts for learning style surveys, academic assesment tools, and trust building activities.

Contents

SECTION II

COMMUNICATION · 57

SECTION III

PROBLEM SOLVING · 93

SECTION IV

CAREER/LEISURE ACTIVITIES · 161

SECTION V

PARENT SUPPORT PROGRAM · *199*

SECTION VI

TRANSITIONAL PLANNING · *243*

BONDING

DISCIPLINE PREVENTION PROGRAM

The Discipline Prevention Program is designed to provide positive rather than punitive discipline. Because of their sensitivity to abusive treatment, at-risk students usually retaliate when it comes to harsh discipline. Therefore, a goal of this program is to change negative behavior into positive behavior. For example, students get attention for positive behavior, gain power by sharing a leadership role, and reverse the revenge motive to empathy by helping instead of hurting others. This reinforcement of positive behavior builds self-esteem.

The following steps encompass the Discipline Prevention Program.

STEP 1: UNDERSTANDING EACH STUDENT'S BEHAVIORAL PROBLEMS

At a preschool meeting (covered in detail in the Introduction to Section 5), the teacher, counselor, parents, and student will meet to:

- identify behavioral problems that have contributed to the student's failure in the classroom
- replace misbehavior with positive classroom behavior via a behavioral contract.

They complete this process by:

✓ Discussing and arriving at the cause of the student's past misbehavior in class.

✓ Identifying and recording this misbehavior on the contract.

✓ Discussing, arriving at, and recording positive behavior to replace misbehavior.

✓ Discussing, arriving at, and recording actions the student will take to execute this positive behavior.

✓ Setting a progress review date to evaluate the student's progress.

✓ Establishing the consequences for not meeting the behavioral goal.

✓ Arriving at a bonus for meeting the behavioral goal, and all parties agree to and sign the contract.

Refer to the sample behavioral contract located in this section.

STEP 2: ESTABLISHING GROUND RULES FOR POSITIVE BEHAVIOR

To complement the behavioral contracts, the teacher will establish the ground rules for behavior in a class activity. This briefing follows the preschool meeting with the parents and is done during the introduction of activity 1 in Section 1. These rules include:

- be a good listener
- show respect for others
- be an active participant
- observe confidentiality

The teacher will carefully explain the purpose of each ground rule and how students will benefit. Refer to the specifics of the ground rules in Activity 1.

STEP 3: SETTING CONSEQUENCES FOR MISBEHAVIOR

The teacher will explain the consequences for misbehavior via a four-step process: (This briefing is done after reviewing the ground rules.)

1st Offense: A reprimand through a positive but firm I-message.

The I-message has three parts:

1. A description of the behavior: *"Joe, when you put down John . . ."*
2. State your feelings: *"I become disturbed . . ."*
3. State the effect of this behavior on the teacher or student: *". . . Because I expect you to treat Joe with respect."*

Final comment: *"Please stop using put-down statements."*

2nd Offense: Conduct a counseling session after school. (Refer to student's behavioral contract.)

3rd Offense: Conduct a parent meeting. (Refer to student's behavioral contract or complete a behavioral contract.)

4th Offense: Suspension from class or drop from the program. (Note: in a special program for at-risk students it is understood that they can be dropped from the program and returned to the regular school program.)

The teacher must make it clear that he/she expects the student to stop misbehavior on the first reprimand. To complement the I-message, the teacher should select a consequence that relates to the infraction such as:

- ✓ A student that is tardy would make up the lost time after school.
- ✓ A student creating a disturbance at the computer center will lose his/her privilege of using a computer for the day.
- ✓ A student printing graffiti on the lavatory wall will scrub off the graffiti.
- ✓ A student losing a book will pay for the lost book, and so on.

STEP 4: INTERVENING TO DISCIPLINE A STUDENT

When intervening to discipline a student, use these basic guidelines:

- Focus on the misbehavior and not the student.
- Deal with the misbehavior immediately; don't allow this behavior to accelerate.
- Be firm and in control in a positive and respectful manner.

The teacher or counselor must adhere to the following *Do's and Don'ts* lists when disciplining at-risk students.

DO'S FOR DISCIPLINING AT-RISK STUDENTS

- Must sincerely care about helping at-risk students succeed in school. (At-risk students will sense your true feelings.)
- Must treat at-risk students with respect. (Respect earns respect in return.)
- Must be compassionate and sincere while being firm and in control.
- Must be positive, patient, and friendly.
- Must be a good role model and practice what you preach.
- Must keep calm and cool and in control of your emotions.

DON'TS FOR DISCIPLINING AT-RISK STUDENTS

- Use a "you" statement or verbal threat (backing an at-risk student into a corner).
- Get into a verbal confrontation with an at-risk student in front of his/her peers.
- Lose your temper and get on the same level as the student.
- Try to dominate a student via a "power trip" motive (I'm always right).
- Use a double standard of "Do what I say" and "Not what I do."
- Treat students differently for breaking the same rule or being inconsistent and unfair.
- Yell at or continuously "bug" students for small infractions rather than quelling a problem immediately.

Characteristics of Attention-Seeking Behavior

An example of a student who seeks attention for his behavior is Jerry. Jerry learned as a child that he could get attention for negative behavior such as crying, not finishing his meal, or disobeying orders. When he attends school, he gets attention by:

- talking in class instead of completing his school assignment
- making weird sounds and funny faces to disturb a classmate
- pushing a classmate as they leave the classroom

The teacher responds by giving Jerry the attention he seeks by reprimanding him in front of his classmates. Jerry's classmates giggle or laugh and he gains further attention accordingly. Through this behavior Jerry has managed to disrupt the class and create a discipline problem for the teacher. When disciplining a student who misbehaves to gain attention, do the following:

- Ignore the behavior if the behavior is incidental and talk to the student about this behavior in private.
- Curb the misbehavior immediately and follow the guidelines for disciplining students.
- Structure the student's activities so he/she will get lots of attention for positive behavior.
- Refer to Step 5, "Facilitating a Collaborative Discipline Process." This process through activities 1 to 7 in Section 1 provides students with attention for positive behavior in class.

Characteristics of Power Behavior

An example of a student who seeks power as a motive for misbehavior is Tony. Tony is very aggressive and flouts others by challenging them with words and actions. He is impressed by the actions of his father and older brother, as they dominate and intimidate others through verbal and physical abuse. His father has been in prison and his brother is a member of a gang. Tony challenges authority figures, such as a classroom teacher, by trying to take charge of the class. Tony particularly likes to challenge a teacher in front of his classmates. When the teacher takes the "bait" and responds to Tony in an argumentative fashion, Tony manipulates the discussion to make the teacher look weak, as he plays the "big man" role. Tony gains the attention he seeks from his fellow students and he becomes a "big shot" in class. Tony is bordering on joining a gang. However, he has leadership potential, and he could become a good student support team leader.

When disciplining a student seeking the "power" motive, do the following:

- Agree with the student if his/her comment has merit.
- If not, inform the student that this is not the time or place to debate an issue; make an appointment to discuss the matter in private.
- Place this student in a leadership role and allow him/her to share in the decision-making process regarding expected behavior in class (as illustrat-

ed in activities 4 and 5 in Section 1). Refer to Step 5, "Facilitating a Collaborative Discipline Process."

Characteristics of Revenge-Seeking Behavior

Betty has been verbally and physically abused by her mother and father since early childhood. They continuously put her down with verbal "you" statements, and slap her in the face when disciplining her. She gains revenge by hurting others through verbal or physical abuse. She is very hostile and aggressive, and she intimidates her classmates. Because of past treatment by her parents, she is very sensitive to the "Don'ts" list for disciplining at-risk students.

When disciplining students who misbehave because of the revenge motive, stress the "Do's" list for disciplining these students. If a student becomes verbally or physically hostile to a teacher or a student, do the following:

- Keep calm and don't retaliate.
- Remove the student to another section of the classroom.
- Attempt to soothe his/her emotions.
- Get the student busy in an activity or just let him/her cool off in isolation.
- Make an appointment to see the student after school to allow adequate time for a productive counseling session as follows:

  Use the communication techniques covered in Section II.

  If the two students are in conflict, use the conflict resolution procedure covered in Section III.

To counter the negativity of students seeking revenge, refer to Step 5 "Facilitating a Collaborative Discipline Process" and utilize activities 1 to 7 in this Section accordingly.

Another intervention technique is to allow the student to "save face." If the student abides by the teacher's reprimand, but has the last word, the teacher does not have to force the issue and create another problem. Both sides win.

For example, the teacher asks Bill to stop disturbing John during a study period. Bill complies, but says something in a low voice. The teacher cannot understand what he is saying, and he can ignore Bill or confront him. If the student is baiting the teacher, the teacher should ignore Bill and make an appointment to talk to him in private.

If a student continues to misbehave after the first reprimand do the following:

- Remove and isolate the student into a designated area in the classroom and keep the student busy with an activity.
- Meet with the student after school for a counseling session.
- If the student continues to misbehave remove him/her from the classroom to a designated area such as: administrator's office, study hall, and so on. If necessary, get help from appointed school staff.

Step 5: Facilitating a Collaborative Discipline Process

Steps 1 to 4 of the Discipline Prevention Program provide a sound basis for handling discipline problems. Initially, the teacher uses these steps for 100% intervention measures to curb discipline problems. However, as students progress through bonding activities, they gradually become responsible for their own behavior, and the teacher's need to intervene lessens. At the conclusion of activity 11, student support teams are trained to be responsible for their behavior individually and as a team. Consequently, the teacher can get out of the disciplinarian role successfully and into the facilitation role. Team leaders play an important role in assisting the teacher to facilitate discipline within their support teams.

The following examples describe how at-risk students learn positive behavior to facilitate this collaborative discipline process.

- A crucial first step in the bonding process is for students and school staff to connect in a positive way. Through activities 1 to 3 students and the teacher become friendly, and they begin to trust and respect each other. Building caring relationships is vital to the emotional well-being of revengeful students. Through caring relationships they will build a basis for positive behavior.

- Via activities 4 and 5 students arrive at behavioral standards for expected behavior and the consequences for misbehavior in class. Students with a power motive have a "say" and share in the decision making process with classmates and the teacher. Students striving for attention provide valuable input and are praised for their contributions. Through this collaborative process, students gain additional trust and respect by valuing the beliefs and opinions of each other. This process complements steps 1 to 4 of the Discipline Prevention Program, as students become involved in the discipline process and the teacher is beginning the facilitation process.

- Through activities 6 and 7 students learn to use build-up statements to compliment each others' special personal qualities. These activities provide lots of positive praise for students requiring attention, and reinforces caring relationships so necessary for revengeful students. These activities enhance self-esteem and trust and respect among students and school staff.

- In activities 8 and 9, permanent student support team members review their long-range educational goals, and they arrive at plans to achieve these goals.

These plans establish a basis for student success in school. At-risk students learn to work cooperatively as members of student support teams.

Students that suffer from fear of failure can become discipline problems as they arrive at excuses for not completing school assignments, and so forth. To overcome this problem, the **steps for success-oriented instruction** are incorporated with activities 8 and 9 as follows:

✓ Assess each student's academic capabilities and learning style and match instruction accordingly.

✓ Use varied and high-interest instructional materials and equipment to match the student's capabilities and learning style.

✓ Provide individualized instruction; students work at their own pace and complete assignments in small increments.

✓ Allow students to master each academic competency before learning advanced competencies.

By completing the above steps, students will succeed in meeting educational goals; consequently, they will build high self-esteem and the confidence to know that they can succeed in school.

- Through activities 10 and 11, student support team members build a support system to help teammates reach their educational goals. This is done by monitoring the behavior of oneself and teammates. Students apply positive peer pressure to motivate teammates to reach their goals and they congratulate each other accordingly. Students with the power motive become excellent team leaders, attention seekers receive much gratification for reaching their goals, and revengeful students belong as capable and respected members of their team. All students gain self-esteem and the confidence to know that they can succeed in school.

ACTIVITY 1

GETTING TO KNOW EACH OTHER

Purpose

To initiate the bonding process among the students and the teacher by getting to know each other.

Skill Development

The student will learn how to:

✓ introduce another student

✓ remember personal things about their partner

✓ remain relaxed during the introduction of a partner

✓ follow the ground rules for conducting an activity

Materials

- A list of questions for the introduction of students
- A list of questions for conducting the discussion
- A list of ground rules for conducting an activity
- A blackboard or paper pad on which to record questions and ground rules
- Chalk or marking pens to print questions and ground rules

Introduction (2 minutes)

The leader will introduce this activity as follows:

1. Tell the students that through this activity they will become acquainted with each other and they will learn their classmates' names.
2. Explain to the students that some of them know each other and others are strangers, and a goal of this activity is to initiate friendships.
3. Inform them that they will learn each others' names, interests, hobbies, and anything else they would like to share about themselves with the class.

Procedure (35 minutes, depending upon the size of the class)

The leader will conduct this activity as follows:

1. Post the ground rules for conducting an activity before beginning this activity.

2. Seat everyone in a full circle.

3. Refer to the list of ground rules and begin by explaining these rules. Pass out handout.

4. Pair off with the student to your left and ask all students to do likewise.

5. Tell them to interview each other for two minutes, and to remember factual things about their partner, because they will introduce their partner to the class.

6. Refer the students to the list of questions as follows:

   - Where do you live and are you from California? (or the name of your state)

   - Do you have any brothers and sisters? What are their names and ages?

   - Do you have any pets? What is your pet's name?

   - What are your favorite things to do?

7. Remind them that they will have two minutes to interview their partner and ask them to begin the interview process.

8. After two minutes have elapsed tell them to switch roles and begin interviewing the other person.

9. After another two minutes stop the activity and begin by introducing your partner to the class.

10. Tell the students to pay close attention to how you introduce your partner; they should follow your example.

Discussion (10 minutes)

The leader will conduct the processing of questions as follows:

1. Divide the class into two separate teams by partners.

2. Explain and refer to the list of ground rules for conducting an activity and review this process as needed.

3. Refer the teams to the following questions and get them started in a discussion.

   - What was the most interesting thing that you learned about your partner?

   - What new thing did you learn about someone you already knew?

   - Ask by a raise of hands: How many of you can remember the names of 5 people, 8 people, 10 or more people?

   - Would anyone like to see how many students you can call by name? If no one volunteers the leader should call out as many names as he/she can remember.

GROUND RULES FOR CONDUCTING A CLASS ACTIVITY

BE A GOOD LISTENER

- Make good eye contact with the speaker

- Don't interrupt the speaker

- Don't talk to others or distract the speaker with funny faces or gestures

SHOW RESPECT TO OTHERS

- Respect the beliefs and opinions of others even when you disagree with them

- Don't put down a classmate through name calling or hurtful gestures

BE AN ACTIVE PARTICIPANT

- Do the activity as well as you can

- Help and support classmates to successfully engage in an activity

OBSERVE CONFIDENTIALITY

- Don't discuss personal issues about your classmates or gossip about others

Appreciation (5 minutes)

Ask each person to say one positive thing about what their partner did or said today. For example, "Wow! John did a great job of remembering the names of my brothers and sisters."

Instructional Tips

1. Before beginning the activity review, the **ground rules** for conducting an activity are as follows:

   - *Be a good listener:* Tell the students to be good listeners by giving the speaker their full attention:

     ✓ make good eye contact with the speaker

     ✓ don't interrupt the speaker

     ✓ don't talk to others or distract the speaker with funny faces or gestures

   - *Show respect to others:* Explain to the students that they should respect the opinions of their peers even when they disagree with them, and they must not put down a teammate by name calling or hurtful gestures.

   - *Be an active participant:* Tell them that each activity will provide them with skills they will use to reach their educational goals and succeed in school. Let them know that an active participant gets involved in team activity by:

     —doing the activity as well as he/she can

     —helping and supporting teammates to engage in an activity successfully

   - *Observe confidentiality:* Explain to the students that things they say of a personal nature must stay within the team, and teammates must not gossip about each other with their peers. To illustrate the meaning of this ground rule, ask the students how they feel when a friend they trust to keep a secret gossips to others about their secret.

2. Explain the consequences for misbehaving or breaking a ground rule. Refer to Step 3, "Setting Consequences for Misbehavior" on page 4.

3. In this activity introducing partners works better than having a student introduce oneself, in that some at-risk students tend to "act out" to show off in front of their classmates or to put the teacher on the spot. Others are too shy to introduce themselves to the class, but they do not mind introducing a classmate.

4. It is recommended to skip the discussion portion of this activity if the students and the teacher are new to each other. Use your professional judgment as to the readiness of your students to perform this part of the activity.

Anticipated Results

The teacher and students have successfully bonded as follows:

- ✓ They know each others' names.
- ✓ They know something personal about each other.
- ✓ They are beginning to become friends.

ACTIVITY 2

SHARING PERSONAL INTERESTS

Purpose

To enhance the bonding process between students and the teacher by becoming better acquainted with each other.

Skill Development

The student will learn how to:

- ✓ share personal interests with others
- ✓ follow directions in an action-oriented activity
- ✓ focus "on-task" to complete an activity
- ✓ interact with others and abide by the ground rules during a discussion period

Materials

- Two sets of 5 x 8 cards with different colored dots drawn on them
- Pens or pencils for the students to use
- A chart illustrating a sample card
- A list of questions for conducting the discussion

Introduction (5 minutes)

The leader will introduce this activity as follows:

1. Tell the students that they will share their personal interests with their classmates, such as their favorite car, food, thing to do, place to visit. Refer to the illustration on the blackboard or paper pad.

2. Inform them that they will have interests in common with fellow students to share and discuss.

3. Tell them that the purpose of this activity is to become better acquainted with each other and to develop friendships.

4. Remind them to do a good job of following directions and abiding by the ground rules so they can complete this activity in an efficient manner.

Procedure (35 minutes)

The leader will conduct this activity as follows:

1. Distribute the cards with different colored dots evenly among the students to form separate teams.

2. Ask the students to print their names just above the dot and an adjective describing the kind of person they are just below the dot (refer to the sample card).

3. Refer to the sample card illustration (on page 16) and tell the students to print the following information:

   - two things they can do well at the bottom of their cards

   - a favorite place to visit at the top of their cards

   - their favorite food on the right side of their cards

   - their favorite car or music on the left side of their cards

4. Do this activity with your students.

5. Ask the students to get up from their chairs and move about the room to find a teammate with the same colored dot and introduce themselves to each other.

6. Tell the students to begin by saying something about their descriptive adjective.

7. Give the students enough time to cover the topic and then ask them to find another teammate with the same colored dot and discuss two things that they can do well.

8. Follow this same rotation while discussing the other parts of the card, through your directions.

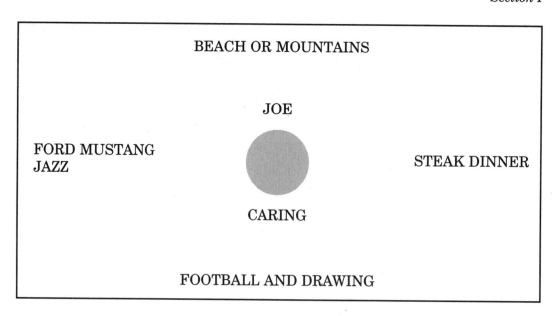

BEACH OR MOUNTAINS

JOE

FORD MUSTANG
JAZZ

STEAK DINNER

CARING

FOOTBALL AND DRAWING

Discussion (10 minutes)

The leader will conduct the processing of questions as follows:

1. Divide the students into teams according to the different colored dots.
2. Refer the teams to the following list of questions and get them started in a discussion.
   - Did you learn anything new about a classmate?
   - Did you find any similarities in interests among classmates?
   - How did it feel to share with others?
   - Did you learn anything new that impressed you about a classmate?

Appreciation (5 minutes)

Ask each person to say one positive thing about what a member of their team did or said today.

Instructional Tips

1. In preparation for this activity, draw a sample card on a paper pad or on the blackboard.
2. When you begin this activity, students will tend to sit in their chairs and wait for someone to come to them to share the information. Therefore, ask the students to stand up and move away from their chairs to find a person with the same colored dot.

3. Do not use red or blue dots or dots associated with gang colors.

4. Model this activity for your students. As you complete a section of the card, instruct students to cover another topic on the card.

5. Your involvement in the activity will help you to monitor and direct the activity in a timely fashion.

6. In preparation for leading the discussion period refer to the guidelines for facilitating a discussion found in the Introduction.

Anticipated Results

The teacher and students are enhancing their bonding process as follows:

✓ They are learning more about each others' personal interests.

✓ They are sharing common interests .

✓ They are beginning to like and respect each other.

ACTIVITY 3

SHARING PERSONAL INFORMATION

Purpose

To intensify the bonding process among the students and the teacher by developing personal relationships.

Skill Development

The student will:

✓ reinforce the learning of how to share personal information with classmates and the teacher

✓ learn how to ask questions and get new information from others

✓ reinforce the practice of following directions and abiding by the ground rules

Materials

- Two sets of *People Sharing Worksheets I and II*
- Pens or pencils for students to use
- A list of questions for conducting the discussion

Introduction (5 minutes)

The leader will introduce this activity as follows:

1. Inform the students that they will share personal information about themselves with their classmates.
2. Tell them they will have some things in common to share with their fellow students and teacher.
3. State that they will discuss new things that are interesting and informative about their teacher and their classmates.
4. Impart to them that by sharing and discussing this latest information about each other that they will find common interests on which to build personal relationships or friendships with others.

Procedure (30 minutes)

The leader will conduct this activity as follows:

1. Distribute People I and People II Sharing Worksheets (located at the end of this activity) evenly among the students to form two separate teams.
2. Direct the students to circulate around the room and locate a teammate with the same numbered worksheet.
3. Ask the students to introduce themselves if they don't know each other, and then share the personal information items on their worksheets in pairs.
4. Give the students 5 minutes to share information with a teammate or teacher, and then ask them to locate another teammate to interview.
5. After 30 minutes have elapsed ask the students to meet with their People I or People II teammates to discuss the activity.

Discussion (10 minutes)

The leader will conduct the processing of questions as follows:
   Refer each team to the following questions and get them started in a discussion.

1. Did you learn anything new about a classmate?
2. Did you find any similarities in information among classmates?
3. Did you learn anything that surprised you about a classmate?
4. What did you like best about this activity?

Appreciation (5 minutes)

Ask each person to say one positive thing about what a member of their teams did or said today.

PEOPLE SHARING WORKSHEET I

1. A person whose birthday is the same as yours.

   Name_____

2. A person who was born in a state other than California.

   Name_____

3. A person who can speak a different language.

   Name_____

4. A person who can cross his or her eyes.

   Name_____

5. A person who likes to play baseball or softball.

   Name_____

6. A person who has more than three brothers and sisters.

   Name_____

7. A person who does not smoke.

   Name_____

8. A person who likes to draw.

   Name_____

9. A person who owns a dog or cat.

   Name_____

10. A person who knows how to play a musical instrument.

    Name_____

PEOPLE SHARING WORKSHEET II

1. A person who has been to a professional baseball game.

   Name _____

2. A person who has more than three animals in his or her home.

   Name _____

3. A person who lives in a home where nobody smokes.

   Name _____

4. A person who is new in town.

   Name _____

5. A person who was born in another country.

   Name _____

6. A person who knows how to tune up a car.

   Name _____

7. A person who likes to go fishing.

   Name _____

8. A person who has been roller skating this past year.

   Name _____

9. A person who does not like to eat garlic.

   Name _____

10. A person who has been water skiing this past summer.

   Name _____

Instructional Tips

1. Begin this activity exactly like activity 2 by asking the students to stand up and move around the room to locate someone with the same *People Sharing* worksheet.

2. Stress the fact that students should make every effort to get an answer for every statement on the worksheet.

3. Participate in this activity so that everyone can get to know each other better, and so you can monitor the timing of this activity in the same fashion as activity 2.

4. Encourage the students to talk to as many students as possible; students will tend to ask their classmates only for information they have received and neglect talking to all students.

Anticipated Results

The teacher and students are intensifying their bonding process as follows:

✓ They are sharing common interests as friends.

✓ They are beginning to trust and respect their classmates and the teacher.

Note: The *People Sharing Worksheets* were designed for students in an urban area in California. You can feel free to change statements to fit your community setting.

ACTIVITY 4

BUILDING POSITIVE STUDENT BEHAVIOR

Purpose

To identify positive and negative behaviors that make the teacher and the students feel comfortable or uncomfortable in the classroom.

Skill Development

The student will learn how to:

✓ express her/his feelings and opinions in an open and positive way

✓ accept and respect the opinions of classmates with differing beliefs

✓ become assertive and express the ideas that are important to him/her

✓ work cooperatively with others to complete a brainstorming session

Materials

- A paper pad or blackboard to print statements on
- Marking pens or chalk for the recorders to use
- A list of questions for conducting the discussion

Introduction (5 minutes)

The leader will introduce this activity as follows:

1. Tell the students that the purpose of this activity is to identify positive and negative behaviors that make them feel comfortable or uncomfortable in the classroom, and to build a foundation for positive student behavior.

2. Tell them they will use this information to arrive at a behavioral code in activity 5.

3. Explain that when students behave in a positive way they treat each other with dignity and respect; but if they tease, put-down, or gossip about others, they will not trust or respect each other.

4. Inform them that when they discuss negative behavior, they must not "name call" or get personal in a negative way. For example, don't mention a classmate by name as in: "John is a jerk when he calls Jack stupid."

Procedure (30 minutes)

The leader will conduct this activity as follows:

1. Divide the students into teams, in advance, according to their compatibility in activities 1 to 3.

2. Ask for a volunteer from each team to be a recorder.

3. Give the recorders two sheets of paper and ask them to label the sheets "comfortable" and "uncomfortable," or ask them to record on the blackboard.

4. Ask each team to brainstorm what makes them feel comfortable in their interaction with classmates and teachers.

5. Ask the recorder to list these items under the "comfortable" heading until ideas become exhausted. Remind the recorder not to write down like items.

6. Ask the teams to brainstorm things that their classmates or teachers do or say that make them uncomfortable in class.

7. Have the recorders list these items under the negative heading.

8. Participate with your students and add items that you believe should be included in these lists.

Discussion (10 minutes)

The leader will conduct the processing of questions as follows:

Refer the teams to their positive and negative lists and ask the following questions. Have the students describe the answers to these questions.

1. Which item makes you feel the most comfortable?

2. Which item makes you feel the most uncomfortable?

3. How do you feel when someone gossips about you?

4. What can you do to make a classmate feel comfortable in class?

Appreciation (5 minutes)

Ask each person to say one positive thing about what a member of their teams did or said today.

Instructional Tips

1. In preparation for this activity use the guidelines found in the Introduction for forming evenly balanced teams.

2. Use strong participants and yourself as role models to guide other students in how to be cooperative and participatory.

3. Make a strong effort to get weak participants involved by:

   - asking for their opinions and ideas

   - letting them know that their contributions are important by using such responses as "good thinking, Mike" or "great idea, Jose"

   - making these students feel like important and valued members of their teams

4. Stress the fact that you and the students must work cooperatively; to illustrate this point, get involved in the discussion by letting students know what makes you feel comfortable or uncomfortable in class.

5. During this activity move from team to team to lead and facilitate as described in the Introduction.

Anticipated Results

The teacher and students have worked cooperatively to achieve the following:

✓ They have arrived at behavior that makes them feel comfortable or uncomfortable in the classroom as a basis for a behavioral agreement.

✓ They are beginning to build trust and respect by valuing and accepting the beliefs and opinions of fellow students and the teacher.

Through this collaborative decision-making process the students and the teacher share in the attention and power to deter misbehavior in the classroom.

ACTIVITY 5

AGREEING ON A BEHAVIORAL CODE

Purpose

To arrive at a code of behavior that becomes the basis for discipline and how to conduct oneself in the classroom.

Skill Development

The student will learn how to:

✓ combine and eliminate behavioral statements that are similar or repetitive, and compile a list of acceptable behavior

✓ prioritize the most important statements to arrive at a behavioral code

✓ practice cooperative interaction through abiding by the ground rules and successfully completing an activity.

Materials

- A paper pad or blackboard to print statements on
- Marking pens or chalk for recorders to use
- A list of questions for conducting the discussion
- Behavioral Contract

Introduction (5 minutes)

The leader will introduce this activity as follows:

1. Tell the students that they will evaluate their lists of positive and negative behaviors and arrive at a code of behavior to abide by in the classroom.

2. Remind them that their beliefs and opinions will be the basis for their behavioral code, and that they will assist you to arrive at a behavioral agreement. Stress the fact that this is a cooperative decision-making effort between students and yourself.

3. Tell them that their behavioral code will be the basis for discipline in their classroom; they will be expected to abide by this code.

4. State that their behavioral guidelines will be a basis to provide positive support for each other in the classroom; through this support they can succeed in school.

Procedure (35 minutes)

The leader will conduct this activity as follows:

1. Ask the students to meet in the same teams as they did for activity 4.

2. Direct them to review their lists of positive and negative items and explain which items are the most important to them. Offer your opinions as well.

3. Ask the students to use a hand vote to select the four most important items from each list.

4. If a team cannot agree on the four most important items, number the items consecutively in order of importance. Ask each student to list the numbers of their four choices on a piece of paper.

5. Recorders must tally the vote.

6. Ask the recorders to print their team's four most important positive items and four most important negative items.

7. Ask the teams to meet back in a full circle to review each team's list of statements.

8. Ask each recorder to tape their team's list of items on a wall in view of the class circle, or copy the items on the blackboard.

9. Monitor the students in a process of combining or eliminating items that are similar or repetitive. This compilation will include a combination of positive and negative statements.

10. As these revisions are made, ask the recorders to record the final statements. These statements comprise the behavioral code. See "Examples of Typical Statements that Form a Behavioral Code" found at the end of this activity (page 27).

Discussion (30 minutes)

Note: It will take another class period to complete this activity.

The leader will conduct this discussion activity as follows:

1. Ask the students to meet in their activity 5 teams.

2. Refer them to the following questions and get them started in a discussion.

   • Which behavioral rule is the most important to you and why?

   • Why are these behavioral rules important to our class?

   • How should we enforce our behavioral rules in class?

   • What should happen to a student who breaks a class rule?

3. Ask each team to brainstorm their ideas generated from the questions in step 2 and record their responses to the last two questions.

4. Ask teams to prioritize top choices.

5. Tell them to meet back in the full class circle.

6. Ask the recorders to tape their team's list of top choices on a wall in view of the class, or to copy the items on the blackboard.

7. Monitor the compilation of items, prioritizing of items, and arrive at the rules for enforcing the behavioral code.

Refer to "Consequences for Not Adhering to the Behavioral Code" found at the end of this activity for more information (page 27).

Instructional Tips

1. You must review the steps in the Activity Procedure and be well prepared for this activity.

2. Your instructions for compiling and prioritizing statements must be succinct and easily understood by your students.

3. If there are time restraints, omit the Appreciation portion of this activity.

Anticipated Results

The teacher and the students have used a collaborative decision-making process to achieve the following results:

✓ They have arrived at a behavioral code to abide by in class.

✓ They have increased trust and respect by respecting and valuing the beliefs and opinions of their classmates and teacher.

✓ They have built a foundation for the collaborative discipline process to deter misbehavior in the classroom.

Examples of Typical Statements That Form a Behavioral Code

✓ Don't say put-down statements to humiliate or embarrass others.

✓ Treat others with dignity and respect.

✓ Don't use facial or hand gestures to disturb or distract others.

✓ Don't gossip about others or repeat things said in confidence.

✓ Don't tease or make fun of what others say or do.

✓ Be a good listener and don't interrupt others.

✓ Accept the ideas, beliefs, and opinions of others.

✓ Smile and say positive things to others.

✓ Don't call each other names, argue, push, or fight.

✓ Follow directions or instructions in class activities.

✓ Be a participant and do tasks to the best of your ability.

Consequences for Not Adhering to the Behavioral Code

When discussing and brainstorming ideas of how to enforce the behavioral code, the teacher should include these suggestions. (Refer to *Step 3: Setting Consequences for Misbehavior* found earlier in Section 1 as a basis for enforcing the behavioral code.)

1st Offense: A positive reprimand by the teacher and student support team members provide input to their team member through positive confrontation. Refer to activity 10 in Section 1. Thus, team members assist the teacher through a collaborative discipline process.

2nd Offense: An after school counseling session with the teacher and counselor.

3rd Offense: Place the student on probation per a behavioral contract.

On the progress review date evaluate if the student is meeting the terms of his/her contract, and either take the student off probation or suspend him/her from class.

4th Offense: Drop the student from class.

To enforce the behavioral contract, student support team members are to apply positive peer pressure to effectively monitor the student's progress. This method of enforcement fits beautifully with the student support system that is outlined in activities 10 and 11.

Students are typically tougher on each other when arriving at their set of consequences. However, the above consequences are fair and through compromise they will accept the above steps as their method for enforcing the behavioral code. The "key" to this process is that the students have a say in the consequences; therefore, they are more apt to adhere to their consequences.

Refer to the sample behavioral contract on the following page.

BEHAVIORAL CONTRACT

NAME _____ DATE _____

TARGET BEHAVIOR: (Replace negative behavior with positive behavior)

NEGATIVE BEHAVIOR: _____

_____

_____

_____

POSITIVE BEHAVIOR: _____

_____

_____

_____

_____ AGREES TO:
       (student's name)

1. _____

2. _____

3. _____

4. _____

5. _____

PROGRESS REVIEW MEETING DATE:_____

BONUS FOR MEETING BEHAVIORAL GOAL: _____

_____

PENALTY FOR NOT MEETING GOAL: _____

_____

WE UNDERSTAND AND AGREE TO THE TERMS OF THIS CONTRACT.

_____ _____ _____ _____
(student's signature) (date) (teacher's signature) (date)

_____ _____ _____ _____
(parent's signature) (date) (counselor's signature) (date)

BUILDING SELF-ESTEEM THROUGH BUILD-UP STATEMENTS

Purpose

To improve a student's self-esteem through build-up statements that reinforce positive behavior in the classroom.

Skill Development

The student will learn how to:

- change put-down statements with positive build-up statements
- use build-up statements to reinforce positive behavior in the classroom

Materials

- Paper pad, marking pens, and scissors
- A chart listing build-up and put-down statements

Introduction (2 minutes)

The leader will introduce this activity as follows:

1. Tell the students that the purpose of this activity is to reinforce the positive behavior of their classmates and improve everyone's self-esteem.
2. Explain to them that this will be done by changing put-down statements into build-up statements.
3. Give examples of build-up statements by referring to the illustrations on the chart.

Procedure (30 minutes)

The leader will conduct this activity as follows:

1. Review the teams from activities 4 and 5, and adjust the students into different teams that appear to be compatible.
2. Ask the students to brainstorm typical put-down statements that teenagers say to each other.

3. Before recording items tell them that no swear words will be used, and to conduct themselves in accordance to their behavior code.

4. Ask for volunteers to act as recorders and have them record these items.

5. After completing the put-down list ask the students to brainstorm build-up statements of opposite meaning. Refer to instructional tips for directions and illustrations of build-up statements.

6. Ask the recorder to draw a line through the put-down message and print build-up statements beside the put-down message.

Discussion (15 minutes)

The leader will conduct the processing of questions as follows:
Refer teams to the following questions and get them started in a discussion. Ask the students to describe their feelings as they answer the questions.

- How do you feel when someone builds you up?
- Can you describe how you feel when someone puts you down?
- How can build-up statements promote trust and respect in class?
- What can we do in class to encourage saying build-up statements to others?
- How can we eliminate saying put-down statements?

Appreciation (5 minutes)

Ask each person to say one positive thing about what a member of their team did or said today.

Instructional Tips

1. When referring to illustrations of opposite put-down and build-up statements, in step 5 of procedures, give the recorders a set of opposite underlined statements, from the list of illustrations, to record on their paper pads.

2. Explain the difference in the meaning of the underlined words as a synonym and an antonym.

3. To help students think of build-up statements, ask them to think of things they say or do to each other that makes them feel special, important, or talented. A smile, pat on the back, or hug are non-verbal build-up statements.

4. If students brainstorm additional build-up statements, per a put-down message, encourage them to respond and ask the recorder to record these statements. Students get more practice saying build-up statements, and they are recognized for their participation.

Examples of Typical Build-Up Statements

- Great effort.
- You're looking good.
- Excellent work.
- Terrific try.
- Marvelous strategy.
- Good thinking.
- Sensational! You're the best at what you do.
- Congratulations! You're a winner.
- Superb! You're outstanding.
- Your smile is friendly.
- Your hair looks great.
- You're a great athlete.
- Stupendous work! You outdid yourself today..
- Wow! You were great today.
- Looking good! Keep up the good work.
- You're the greatest.
- You're eyes are beautiful.

Examples of Put-Down Statements

- You stink!
- Idiot! get out of my way.
- Dummy! can't you do anything right.
- You're stupid.
- You're a fool.
- You're a jerk.
- You suck.
- You're a dipstick.

(continued on next page)

Examples of Put-Down Statements *(continued)*

- Jerk! Get out of my face.
- You're a dirty rat.
- You're a loser.
- You're nasty.
- You're no good at anything.
- You're nuts.
- Crackpot! Stay away from me.
- Get lost stupid..

Anticipated Results

The teacher and the students have enhanced bonding, trust, respect, and self-esteem among themselves by praising others through build-up statements that reinforce positive behavior in the classroom.

ACTIVITY 7

SHARING APPRECIATION FOR OTHERS

Purpose

To enhance the student's self-esteem by showing appreciation for his or her special personal qualities.

Skill Development

The student will learn how to:

- validate the special qualities of others
- recognize the difference between a clear or fuzzy validation
- appreciate the unique personal qualities of different classmates

Materials

- Paper plates and pens or pencils
- A chart with an illustration of both a clear and a fuzzy validation

Introduction (5 minutes)

The leader will introduce this activity as follows:

1. Explain that the purpose of this activity is to show our appreciation for others' special qualities, such as being considerate, friendly, or a helping person.
2. Inform them that every person in class is worthy of their attention, consideration, and respect.
3. Tell them that when they validate classmates, they are telling them they are special.
4. Explain to the students that a build-up statement is an example of how they can validate another person in a positive way.
5. Tell them that when they validate others their validation should be clear and not "fuzzy."
6. Refer to the illustration and explain the difference between a clear and fuzzy validation.

Procedure (25 minutes)

The leader will conduct this activity as follows:

1. Seat the class in a full circle.
2. Pass out paper plates to every student and staff member and ask them to put their name in the middle of their plate.
3. Ask each person to pass their plate to the person to his/her left and then print a positive word or statement on that person's plate.
4. Ask everyone to continue passing the plates to their left and follow this process until all of the plates have gone around the circle and back to the original owner.

Discussion (15 minutes)

The leader will conduct the processing of questions as follows:

1. Divide the students into teams.

2. Refer the teams to the following questions and get them started in a discussion.

   • How did it feel to be validated by your classmates?

   • How did you feel when you validated another person?

   • How does being validated increase your self-esteem and make you feel good about yourself?

   • Why is it important for us to tell others what we admire and appreciate about them?

Appreciation (10 minutes)

Ask each person to look at their validation plate and pick out the word or statement they like the best and why.

Instructional Tips

1. Before you begin this activity, record the following examples of "clear" and "fuzzy" validations on a paper pad or on the blackboard. During the introduction, refer to the following examples:

   • **Fuzzy validation:** "You look great"

   • **Clear validations:** "Your hair looks great" "Your smile looks great" "Your eyes are beautiful"

   Continue by explaining that a clear validation is very specific and compliments the other person for his/her personal qualities. Remind the students that before they validate someone, think specifically about that person's special qualities such as a good sense of humor, great smile, beautiful eyes, strong muscles, skill in mathematics, or being a good baseball player.

2. In preparation for this activity use the guidelines for placing students on teams and place students on teams in preparation for the discussion period.

3. At the end of this activity give the students a piece of paper and ask them to print the name of one or more classmates they trust and respect. Use this information to assist you in arranging permanent teams for activity 8.

Anticipated Results

This activity will enhance bonding, trust and respect, and self-esteem among students and the school staff by displaying wholehearted appreciation for others' special personal qualities.

SETTING WEEKLY ACADEMIC GOALS

Purpose

To guide students in how to select and achieve their weekly academic goals.

Skill Development

The student will learn how to:

- set weekly educational goals
- arrive at a plan for completing these goals
- work cooperatively in student support teams to arrive at academic goals and plans

Materials

- A paper pad or blackboard on which to print statements
- Marking pens or chalk for the recorders to use
- Goal Form
- Long-Range Educational Goals Form for the students to use and refer to during the activity (Each student brings his/her own Long-Range Goals Form.)

Introduction (3 minutes)

The leader will introduce this activity as follows:

1. Tell the students that they will reach their long-range educational goal through meeting a series of weekly academic goals.
2. State that they must select their own academic goals and that these goals must be within their ability to attain.
3. Explain that the purpose of this activity is to set weekly academic goals and arrive at steps to achieve these goals.

Procedure (45 minutes)

The leader will conduct this activity as follows:

1. Inform the students that today they will meet in their permanent student support teams.

2. Read off the names of students and place them as a team around a table or in a cluster of desks arranged in a circle.

3. Ask the students to bring their Long-Range Educational Goals Form that states their long-range educational goal with them to this activity.

4. Pass out Goal Forms to team members and ask them to record their long-range educational goal on step 1 of their goal form.

5. Ask each student to share his or her educational goal with their teammates.

6. After this discussion, ask them to record on step 2 of their goal form the following statement: "To successfully complete my daily and weekly academic assignment."

7. Remind them they will need to successfully complete their weekly assignments to eventually reach their long-range educational goal.

8. Ask the recorders to copy step 3 (steps to take) as a heading on a paper pad or on the blackboard.

9. Ask teams to brainstorm steps that each student must take to reach his/her weekly goal.

10. Have the recorders record the brainstorming ideas under the step 3 heading.

11. Tell the students to use the same brainstorming procedure to cover steps 4 and 5 on their goal form.

12. Remind them that the deadline for reaching their goal (step 6) is weekly.

Discussion

At the conclusion of this activity, if time permits, ask a representative from each team to share their goal setting information with the other teams.

Appreciation (omit)

Instructional Tips

1. Refer to the Introduction on Implementing Student Support Teams for instructions on how to form permanent teams.

2. As the recorder records brainstorming ideas under the heading for steps 3, 4, and 5, students can copy these ideas on their goal forms, or a teammate could take notes on a goal form and xerox copies for his/her teammates.

3. When utilizing this activity within a self-contained classroom, students and parents have met in preparation for this activity to:

   • arrive at an Individual Education Plan, and

   • a long-range educational goal.

   Refer to Section 5 in order to learn how this process works.

GOAL FORM

NAME _____ DATE _____

STEPS

1. Record your long-range educational goal.

    _____

    _____

2. Record your short-term weekly academic goal.

    _____

    _____

3. Record steps to take to reach your weekly academic goal.

    _____

    _____

    _____

    _____

    _____

4. Record the barriers that could keep you from reaching your weekly goal.

    _____

    _____

    _____

    _____

5. Record ways to overcome your barriers.

    _____

    _____

6. Set a deadline for reaching your goal.

    _____

4. When students meet in a counseling group or an elective class, you can opt to have the students record on step 1 of their goal forms: "To graduate from high school" as their long-range educational goal.

- Next, ask the students the following question: What are the benefits of graduating from high school?

- Conduct a discussion around this question and add your own comments. For example, you could mention the need to have advanced education to qualify for the jobs of today and in the future.

- Continue this activity by following the directions given in the Activity Procedure and Instructional Tips, in that the rest of this activity follows the original format.

Anticipated Results

Student Support Team members assisted each other to arrive at plans to achieve their weekly academic goal by:

- ✓ having a good understanding of their own and their teammates' goals
- ✓ understanding the need for good work habits and attitudes to reach their weekly goals.

By arriving at educational goals, student support team members have established a basis for achieving academic success.

ACTIVITY 9

APPLYING ACADEMIC GOALS TO COMPLETE SCHOOL ASSIGNMENT

Purpose

To direct the students in how to apply their academic goals and plans to successfully complete their academic assignments.

Skill Development

The student will:

- ✓ learn how to apply weekly academic goals to complete school assignments
- ✓ reinforce the need to apply good work habits and attitudes to meet educational goals

Materials

- Goal Form and Educational Contract for each student
- pens or pencils
- weekly academic contract

Introduction (2 minutes)

The leader will introduce the activity as follows:

1. Explain that today they will learn how to apply their weekly goals and plans to successfully complete their educational contracts and academic assignments.
2. Reinforce the need to successfully complete their weekly school assignments in order to eventually reach their long-range educational goal.

Procedure (35 minutes)

Note: This procedure is used for a self-contained classroom. Refer to instructional tips for counseling group procedure.

Conduct this activity as follows:

1. Meet separately with each team.
2. Ask team members to bring their goal forms to this activity.
3. Give each student a copy of his or her completed weekly educational contract, or instruct them on how to complete their contracts during class time.
4. Refer team members to the completed steps on their goal forms (from activity 8) and lead a discussion around the need to apply these steps to complete their weekly education contracts. For relevancy, ask the students to look at a specific subject area assignment on their contracts, and think in terms of how they will apply these steps to complete this specific assignment.
5. Ask each student to select a step and describe how he or she can apply this step to successfully complete the school assignment.
6. Repeat this process so that every student will get an opportunity to speak.

Discussion (10 minutes)

The leader will conduct this discussion as follows:
Refer the team to the following statements and lead a discussion.

- Describe the kind of attitude you must have to complete your weekly goals.
- Describe the kind of work habits you must employ to meet your weekly goals.

Appreciation (5 minutes)

Ask each member of the team to say one positive thing about what a member of their team did or said today.

Instructional Tips

1. An educational contract is recommended as an excellent tool for monitoring and evaluating academic assignments in a self-contained classroom. Within a self-contained classroom each student's curriculum is individualized; therefore, each course of study will vary from student to student. Depending upon your mode of operation, you can prepare each student's daily or weekly course of study assignments in one of the following ways:

   - Design a daily or weekly schedule of subject area assignments for each student during after school hours, and pass out these assignments to the students during class time.

   - Meet weekly with each student or a group of students with the same course schedule, and give them their course of study assignments to record on their contracts during class time.

   - Meet daily with students that have the same course of study schedule, and give them their daily assignments to record on their contracts during class time. **Note:** There are five spaces marked Monday through Friday for each subject on the proposed contract. See contract on following page.

   The advantages and disadvantages of the above approaches are obvious, and you can decide which method best meets your management style.

2. Explanation of the Proposed Weekly Contract

   The following information will explain how to complete and use the proposed weekly contract:

   - Begin by recording the name of the student and the dates of the contract (Monday through Friday).

   - List the exact course title under the course title heading.

   - Record a description of the daily assignments such as Chapter 2, page 10, in *American Continents*.

   - If you use variable credits include the number of hours or minutes it will take to complete the assignment.

   - After completing the above portions of the contract, give the students their course of study assignments and ask them to sign their contracts.

   - After the students have completed their assignments, evaluate their lessons and place a letter grade or percent score in the evaluation section of the contract.

WEEKLY ACADEMIC CONTRACT

NAME _____

DATES _____ TO _____

COURSE TITLE	DAY	DESCRIPTION OF ASSIGNMENTS—HOURS	EVALUATION	COMP. HOURS			FINAL GRADE/CREDITS
					Total Hours	Accum Hours	
	M						GRADE
	T						
	W						
	Th						
	F						CREDIT
	M						GRADE
	T						
	W				Total Hours	Accum Hours	
	Th						
	F						CREDIT
	M						GRADE
	T						
	W				Total Hours	Accum Hours	
	Th						
	F						CREDIT
	M						GRADE
	T						
	W				Total Hours	Accum Hours	
	Th						
	F						CREDIT
	M						GRADE
	T						
	W				Total Hours	Accum Hours	
	Th						
	F						CREDIT

I agree to complete the above assigned work: _____

Student Signature

Total Weekly Hours _____

ADA _____

- If you use variable credits list the number of hours or minutes it took to complete each daily assignment under the completed hours (Comp. Hours) section of the contract. Record the total weekly hours completed for each subject under the "Total Hours" heading.
- When a student completes a subject, place the final grade and credits under the "Final Grade/Credit" heading
- If Average Daily Attendance (ADA) is based upon productive hours of assigned work (which is done for independent study classes in California), record the weekly hours and ADA figures in the appropriate space.

The contract on the previous page was designed for a self-contained classroom using a variable credit system. Educators can adapt this contract to meet their specific needs.

3. Activity procedure for a counseling group is as follows:
   - Follow the same initial steps as described for the self-contained classroom.
   - Instead of referring students to an educational contract, you will reference to their specific subject areas or school assignments.
   - Refer students to the completed steps on their goal forms and lead a discussion about how to apply these steps to successfully complete their school assignments.
   - For relevancy ask each student to select a specific step and describe how to apply this step to successfully complete a particular academic assignment.
   - Repeat this process so that every student will get a chance to speak.
   - During the discussion period encourage students to compare ideas and share opinions, to get new ideas about how to succeed in school. In this instance, students will apply these ideas to various classes that they attend rather than to an educational contract.

Anticipated Results

Student support team members aid their teammates to apply weekly educational goals and plans to successfully complete school lessons by:

✓ applying good work habits and attitudes to successfully complete mathematics or history lessons, and so forth, or academic contracts.

Students enduring the "fear of failure" syndrome are placed on a success-oriented instructional program to:

✓ complete their educational assignments or weekly contracts successfully.

Refer to the **steps for success-oriented instruction** on the page prior to activity 1.

ACTIVITY 10

BUILDING A POSITIVE STUDENT SUPPORT SYSTEM

Purpose

To provide a support system whereby student support team members monitor their behavior per the behavioral code, to help teammates attain their educational goals.

Skill Development

The students will learn how to:

✓ monitor their own behavior and the behavior of teammates

✓ support their teammates to successfully complete educational goals

✓ arrive at a team agreement for supporting each other

✓ tutor and study together via a cooperative education format

Materials

- A paper pad or blackboard on which to print statements
- Marking pens or chalk for the recorders to use
- Team Agreement Forms
- Pens or pencils

Introduction (3 minutes)

The leader will conduct this activity as follows:

1. Tell the students that the purpose of this activity is to build a support system, whereby they help each other meet their educational goals.

2. Stress the fact that team members will learn to monitor their own behavior and the behavior of their teammates.

3. Remind them that this behavior will transfer into good work habits and attitudes which are necessary to reach weekly academic goals.

Procedure (45 minutes)

The leader will conduct this activity as follows:

1. Meet separately with each team while the other teams are studying cooperatively to complete their course assignments.

2. Ask for a volunteer to record two headings on a paper pad or blackboard as follows: Do's—How to provide positive support to a teammate, Don'ts—How to deter a teammate's academic progress.

3. Ask team members to brainstorm items to list under each category and have a recorder record these items.

4. Facilitate this activity by encouraging students to include: working cooperatively to achieve individual and team goals, giving and receiving positive confrontation, changing negative behavior, and tutoring each other (see instructional tips).

5. Summarize the main ideas from both lists and compile one list.

6. Tell the team members that this list is their team agreement, and by fulfilling this agreement they will help themselves to successfully complete their weekly goals.

7. Ask team members what the consequences should be for a teammate who fails to abide by their team agreement.

8. Ask the recorder to list these items on a paper pad or blackboard.

9. Facilitate this activity so that the consequences are equal to the consequences for not abiding by class behavioral code, per activity 5.

10. Pass out team agreement forms to team members and have them complete these forms.

11. Remind the team members that it is their responsibility to abide by their team agreement. Summarize the positive reasons why this is important and the negative consequences for failure to adhere to their agreement.

Note: This activity takes a full class period to complete. However, the instructor can take an additional class period, or a portion of another class period, to include the discussion and appreciation sections of this activity.

Discussion (omit)

Appreciation (omit)

Instructional Tips

1. During the facilitation of this activity participate by adding items to the Do's and Don'ts lists such as:

   • Include positive confrontation under the Do's list. Explain that positive confrontation means to confront, in a positive way, a teammate that is

TEAM AGREEMENT

_____ agrees to abide by the following team agreements:
      name

- _____

- _____

- _____

- _____

- _____

- _____

- _____

- _____

- _____

- _____

- _____

- _____

Failure to abide by this team agreement will result in the following consequences:

- _____

- _____

- _____

- _____

_____   _____

Team Member's Signature   Date

not practicing good work habits, attitudes, or positive communication per the behavioral code. Agree that it is okay to confront others in a positive way.

- Illustrate how to use an I-message to confront a teammate such as "John, please quit talking, I can't concentrate on my math because you are making too much noise." Put this example on a paper pad to refer to during this illustration.

- Under the Don'ts list include not using "you" statements or put-down statements to confront or offend a teammate. Illustrate the difference between using an I-message vs. using a "you" message. Refer to activities 8 and 9 in Section II.

- Explain that changing negative behavior has to do with using build-up statements to replace put-down statements (refer to activity 6), and practicing good work habits and attitudes instead of fooling around and not completing course assignments.

2. If you decide to use a team agreement form, make a copy of each team's signed agreement and keep these student agreement forms on file for future reference. Ask the students to keep their original copy at their desk as a reminder of how to behave during team interaction.

3. When working with a counseling group or an elective class, complete activity 10 as is, with the following addition—ask student support team members to assist teammates as peer helpers or mentors outside of class to:

- succeed in classes where they are having difficulty

- become actively engaged in after-school leisure or career activities

- cope with personal problems

Anticipated Results

Student support team members build a support system to help each other achieve their educational goals by:

✓ monitoring the behavior of oneself and teammates per the behavioral code and team agreement

✓ supporting and assisting teammates through positive confrontation and cooperative education to complete their weekly educational goals.

Through this support system the teacher and student support teams implement the collaborative discipline process to deter disciplinary problems in the classroom.

ACTIVITY 11

ATTAINING EDUCATIONAL GOALS VIA POSITIVE PEER PRESSURE

Purpose

To guide student support teams in how to apply positive peer pressure, via a peer audit, to attain their educational goals.

Skill Development

The student will learn how to:

✓ conduct a peer audit

✓ apply positive peer pressure to motivate teammates

✓ apply positive reinforcement to raise the self-esteem of teammates

Materials

- Weekly Peer Audit Forms
- Tally sheet for peer audit
- Progress report and Self-Audit Form
- Pens and pencils

Introduction (5 minutes)

The leader will introduce this activity as follows:

1. Inform the students that today they will learn how to complete a peer audit.

2. Tell them that the purpose of this audit is for them to evaluate their work habits, attitudes, and communication skills to determine the following:

   - Are they providing positive support, per their team agreement, or are they a negative influence to team members?

   - Are teammates working diligently to reach their educational goals?

3. Remind them that the results of the peer audit will tell them if they are succeeding in school as an individual and a team member.

Procedure (30 minutes)

The leader will conduct the activity as follows:

1. Conduct a class meeting by seating students in a circle.

2. Pass out a copy of the Weekly Peer Audit Form to everyone in class.

3. Review the categories of the peer audit form—work habits, attitudes, and communication skills.

4. Answer questions that students have about these categories.

5. Explain the point system and how they will rate each others' behavior during the week, and answer the questions accordingly.

6. Inform students that they will meet as a team each week to review their peer audits.

Procedure II (35 minutes)

After the students have completed the peer audit forms, the leader will pick them up and tally the scores. If an educational contract is used, bring a copy of each student's completed weekly contract to this meeting. Then the leader will meet separately with each team to:

1. Review the peer audit results of a student support team.

2. Share the relationship of the student's audit score with his/her results on their educational contract. Students scoring high on their peer audit invariably succeed in completing their academic goals.

3. Congratulate the team members that score high on their peer audits and educational contracts and encourage teammates to applaud his/her efforts.

4. Tell the team members that a goal for their team is for everyone to successfully complete their weekly goals.

5. Inform them that their team will receive an award when all members reach their weekly academic goals, such as:

   - team name recognition or displaying a photograph of successful teams through bulletin board displays

   - special buttons to wear, saying "Number One," and so on

   - special recognition through school newspapers or newsletters

   - free coupons from fast food restaurants for pizza, and so forth (some restaurants give free food coupons for special programs or for worthy causes)

   - special class privileges such as getting a free class period to view an educational videotape of their choice

Note: Teachers and counselors should use their imagination and creativity when selecting awards (given their resources), and should vary awards from time to time.

Discussion (10 minutes)

The leader will guide the processing of questions as follows:
Refer the team to the following questions and lead a discussion.

1. How did it feel to be applauded for meeting your goals?
2. How did your teammates help you reach your weekly goals?

Appreciation (5 minutes)

Ask each person to say one positive thing about what a team member did or said today.

Instructional Tips

1. Record the names of teammates on weekly peer audit forms (covering each team) and reproduce enough copies for all students, or ask the students to legibly print the names of teammates on their audit forms. Remind them to include their name on the form and to rate themselves.

2. To properly facilitate a peer audit, pass out the peer audit forms to the students each Monday; ask the students to rate his/her behavior and the behavior of teammates (Monday through Friday). On Friday, pick up completed audits from each team member and paper-clip team scores together as one unit.

3. List team members' names on a tally sheet.

4. Pull the scores from each team member's Peer Audit Forms and place these scores in the attitude, work habit, and communication sections of the tally sheet. For example, a team of six will have six scores in each section of the tally sheet. See tally sheet form at the end of this activity.

5. Total each member's scores for each of the three sections and divide by the number of team members to get an average score for each category.

6. Per the directions in the activity procedure, encourage teammates to applaud each other for high scores. Act as a role model by saying "Let's applaud John for a great effort."

7. It is important to give team awards. This will motivate team members to support and help each other to reach team goals as well as individual goals.

Explanation of Weekly Peer Audit

The following information will explain how to complete and use the peer audit form:

1. Explain that Excellent or a rating of 5 indicates that a student is displaying outstanding work habits, attitudes, and communication skills; a good rating is a score of 4 which is an above average score; an average rating is a score of 3; a poor rating is a score of 2 which indicates the student is putting forth very little effort; and failure to participate is a rating of 1.

2. Tell the students that as they rate themselves and their teammates, they will circle one of the above numbers as indicated above.

3. Ask each student to record his/her name and date at the top of the form, and be prepared to turn in a completed audit form each Friday.

4. When completing the tally sheet, identify each team by placing a number after the term (team) in the upper right hand corner of the form.

5. At the bottom of the tally sheet, record how each team member rated himself or herself, in each category, to get a comparison of individual and team scores. See the sample *Tally Sheet* and *Weekly Peer Audit* following this activity.

Instructions for Conducting a Peer Audit in a Counseling Group or Elective Class

1. When conducting a peer audit in a counseling group or an elective class, team members will audit their behavior during student support team activities. They will follow the previous directions given in the activity procedure and instructional tips.

2. To get an additional rating as to how they are doing in their other subject area classes, students will use the Progress Report and Self-Audit Form as follows: (refer to this form as you review these directions)

   - The students will rate themselves by placing a check mark under the "Student" heading for each category such as: *Academic, Work Habits, Attitude,* and *Communication,* and opposite the rating scale of *Excellent, Good, Average, Poor,* and *Fail.*

   - Next, the students will meet with their subject area teachers each Thursday, and ask each teacher to rate them by placing a check mark under the heading "Teacher" for each category such as: *Academic, Work Habits, Attitude,* and *Communication,* and opposite the rating scale of *Excellent, Good, Average, Poor,* and *Fail.* Teachers should sign this form in ink.

   - The student will bring this completed audit form to the weekly peer audit review meeting on Fridays. This meeting is conducted as described in the activity procedure and instructional tips for activity 11.

3. To get a comparison between the audit scores and the student's subject area letter grades, the teacher will ask students to bring their quarterly and semester grade reports to the appropriate peer review meeting. Accordingly, they will make a comparison and react as follows:

   - They will congratulate the students who attain high scores and letter grades.
   - They will discuss how they can support or assist a teammate who is making poor grades.

Anticipated Results

Student support team members apply positive peer pressure to motivate their teammates to successfully accomplish their academic goals by:

✓ using a peer audit to enhance good work habits and attitudes needed to succeed academically

✓ congratulating team members for their high achievement in the peer audit and academic assignments. This success and positive reinforcement breeds confidence and raises the student's self-esteem.

The peer audit process complements the student support system to improve the execution of the collaborative discipline process.

SUMMARY

Through activities 8 to 11 students have learned how to function as permanent members of student support teams, and as teammates they have accomplished the following:

- identified their educational goals
- designed plans to achieve these goals
- learned how to use positive peer pressure to generate positive behavior as a vehicle that motivates teammates to successfully meet their educational goals.

Through this training, student support teams function effectively for the remainder of the school year as:

- cooperative learning study teams
- student support teams to facilitate activities in Sections 2–6 as needed.

Team leaders emerge and they assist the teacher in facilitating these activities.

The *Student Teams Achievement Division* (STAD) is recommended as the cooperative learning method to use for study teams. In a subject area class, the teacher presents a lesson, and the student support team members assist each other until all the members have mastered the lesson. They take the test or quiz individually. In a self-contained classroom that uses individualized instruction, team members pair off or tutor each other to master a lesson. Or students working at the same grade level form a study team to cover the same lesson and they use the STAD method. Refer to Section 3 for specific information about the cooperative learning instructional methods.

Through successful completion of activities 1 to 10 in Section 1, student support team members gain trust and respect for each other, the teacher, and the counselor. Consequently, team members feel an obligation to be honest in their evaluation and completion of the peer audit. Guidance by team leaders and the teacher and/or counselor will also promote honesty in completion of the peer audit.

Note: It has been the author's experience that the peer audit has been the most powerful tool of this program in establishing positive peer pressure to achieve good work habits, attitudes, and communication skills.

WEEKLY PEER AUDIT

DATE_____   RATER_____

	NAMES		RATING	
		Excellent	5 4 3 2 1	Needs Improvement
ATTITUDE		Excellent	5 4 3 2 1	Needs Improvement
		Excellent	5 4 3 2 1	Needs Improvement
Is a friend.		Excellent	5 4 3 2 1	Needs Improvement
Is supportive to others.		Excellent	5 4 3 2 1	Needs Improvement
Treats others with respect.		Excellent	5 4 3 2 1	Needs Improvement
Is an honest and trustworthy person.		Excellent	5 4 3 2 1	Needs Improvement
Puts forth his/her best effort.		Excellent	5 4 3 2 1	Needs Improvement
		Excellent	5 4 3 2 1	Needs Improvement
		Excellent	5 4 3 2 1	Needs Improvement
WORK HABITS		Excellent	5 4 3 2 1	Needs Improvement
		Excellent	5 4 3 2 1	Needs Improvement
Gets on task to complete study assignments.		Excellent	5 4 3 2 1	Needs Improvement
Does not distract others during study time by talking, visiting, or bizarre behavior.		Excellent	5 4 3 2 1	Needs Improvement
		Excellent	5 4 3 2 1	Needs Improvement
Works cooperatively to help others.		Excellent	5 4 3 2 1	Needs Improvement
		Excellent	5 4 3 2 1	Needs Improvement
		Excellent	5 4 3 2 1	Needs Improvement
COMMUNICATION SKILLS		Excellent	5 4 3 2 1	Needs Improvement
		Excellent	5 4 3 2 1	Needs Improvement
Is a good listener.		Excellent	5 4 3 2 1	Needs Improvement
Does not interrupt others.		Excellent	5 4 3 2 1	Needs Improvement
Does not put-down others or gossip about others.		Excellent	5 4 3 2 1	Needs Improvement
Helps teammates with school assignments or peer problems.		Excellent	5 4 3 2 1	Needs Improvement
		Excellent	5 4 3 2 1	Needs Improvement
		Excellent	5 4 3 2 1	Needs Improvement

TALLY SHEET FOR PEER AUDIT

Team_____ Date_____ 12/12/88

Name	Attitude Score	Ttl	Ave	Work Habits Score	Ttl	Ave	Communication Score	Ttl	Ave
Del	5 5 3 2 4 4	23	3.8	5 5 4 4 4 4	26	4.3	5 5 4 4 3 3	34	4
Randy	2 3 2 4 2 3	16	2.6	2 2 2 3 2 2	13	2.1	2 2 2 2 2 2	12	2
Anna	5 5 4 3 2 2	21	3.5	5 5 2 3 4 3	22	3.6	5 5 3 4 3 4	24	4
Josh	5 5 4 5 3 5	27	4.5	5 5 5 4 5 4	28	4.6	5 5 4 5 5 5	29	4.8
Sandy	5 5 4 5 5 4	28	4.6	5 5 5 4 4 4	27	4.5	5 5 5 5 5 5	30	5
Scott	2 4 2 3 3 3	17	2.8	2 1 2 3 3 2	12	2	3 2 3 3 2 1	14	2.3

Rater's Score

Name			
Del	5	5	5
Randy	3	2	3
Anna	5	5	5
Josh	5	5	5
Sandy	5	5	5
Scott	3	2	5

TALLY SHEET FOR PEER AUDIT

Team_____

Date_____

NAME	ATTITUDE SCORE	TTL	AVE	WORK HABITS SCORE	TTL	AVE	COMMUNICATION SCORE	TTL	AVE

RATER'S SCORE

PROGRESS REPORT AND SELF AUDIT

NAME _____

DATES _____ TO _____

TEACHER (Signature)	SUBJECT	ACADEMIC		WORK HABITS		ATTITUDE		COMMUNICATION		
		Teacher	Student	Teacher	Student	Teacher	Student	Teacher	Student	Excellent / Good / Average / Poor / Fail
										Excellent / Good / Average / Poor / Fail
										Excellent / Good / Average / Poor / Fail
										Excellent / Good / Average / Poor / Fail
										Excellent / Good / Average / Poor / Fail
										Excellent / Good / Average / Poor / Fail
										Excellent / Good / Average / Poor / Fail

GRADING CODE: Excellent = A–Grade Good = B–Grade Average = C–Grade Poor = D–Grade Fail = F–Grade

COMMUNICATION

INTRODUCTION

In Section II, teachers and counselors are given the tools needed to teach students positive communication skills. These skills are necessary to implement the classroom behavioral code properly. As the basis for expected behavior in the classroom, the behavior code specifies that students must adhere to the following guidelines:

- Treat classmates with dignity and respect.
- Respect the beliefs, ideas, and opinions of others.
- Relate to classmates and teachers in a positive and friendly manner.
- Adhere to the basics of good communication skills such as properly conversing, listening, observing, and interpreting when communicating with others.

To implement these guidelines, teachers and counselors will teach students how to:

✓ replace put-down statements with build-up statements

✓ start a conversation and be a good listener

✓ observe and interpret verbal and nonverbal patterns of communication

✓ listen from the heart and display empathy

✓ use positive *I-messages* to replace negative You messages

✓ use assertive behavior to resist negative peer pressure

Consequently, practicing these positive communication skills in the classroom enhances the facilitation of the Behavioral Code. Successful implementation of the behavioral code should improve the collaborative discipline process since students and teachers work cooperatively to quell disciplinary problems.

Team members are learning these communication skills in order to monitor themselves and create an environment where everyone can get something academic accomplished. As students become responsible for their own behavior in the classroom, the teacher is free to teach rather than spend valuable time disciplining students. This is the "key" to the collaborative discipline process.

The sequential elements that provide a structure for responsible student behavior in the classroom are as follows:

- The behavioral code that specifies expected student behavior in the classroom (activity 5, Section I)

- The facilitation of the behavioral code through a student support system (activity 10, Section I)

- The implementation of the behavioral code through the learning and practicing of good communication skills (Section II)

For example, an important aspect of the team agreement, (activity 10, Section I) is monitoring each others' behavior. To accomplish this task, activity 8 in Section II teaches students how to use *I-messages* to confront a teammate in positive ways. Communication skills should be covered at the conclusion of activity 11, Section I.

Other ways that this communication unit can be used are as follows:

- The teacher or counselor can use these positive communication techniques to enhance instruction and conduct counseling sessions after school.

- Teammates can use these positive communication skills to console each other in time of need. Barbara Varenhorst, the founder of "Peer Helpers" at Palo Alto High School in California, concluded that most students talk to peers about personal problems instead of talking to adults. Therefore, these skills improve this support process.

- Students can use these skills to communicate in a positive way with their classmates, friends, parents, and community members.

These communication skills can also be used to train voluntary peer helpers or peer mentors in an after-school program to assist freshmen or at-risk students in their adjustment to high school. Refer to a reference in the back of this guide for information on how to start a peer helpers' program called *Curriculum Guide for Student Peer Counseling* (1980) by Barbara Varenhorst.

Another goal of Section II is to provide students with the communication capability to support their teammates in successfully completing their educational goals.

Section II can stand by itself when used by any classroom teacher to prevent or troubleshoot communication problems in a difficult classroom setting. For example, in a biology class that requires small groups to complete lab projects, the students are uncommunicative and disorganized. In this instance, the teacher spends most of his/her time negotiating squabbles, disciplining students, and so forth. The 10 activities in Section II produce a structure of expected behavior where students can learn to be civil to one another so that they can work cooperatively to learn biology. The teacher should be explicit and say to his/her class, "We are taking 10 class periods to practice some communication skills that will help us respect one another so that we can get back to learning biology."

ACTIVITY 1

PRACTICING REAL-LIFE ROLES

Purpose

To understand how to practice a real-life role.

Skill Development

The student will learn how to :

✓ understand the guidelines for role practicing/role playing

✓ role practice by practicing a real-life situation with a teammate

✓ display empathy in an appropriate situation

Materials

- *Guidelines for Role Practicing* handout

Introduction (3 minutes)

The leader will introduce this activity as follows:

1. Tell the students that today they will learn how to role practice.
2. Explain that the term role practice is used instead of role playing because they will be practicing real-life roles and not playacting.
3. Inform them that they will be practicing situations they come in contact with at school, home, and on the streets.
4. Tell them they will use role practicing to learn and practice skills that will help them relate better to peers, teachers, and parents.

Procedure (30 minutes)

The leader will conduct the activity as follows:

1. Pass out copies of the role practicing guidelines to all students.
2. Explain these guidelines and answer questions.
3. Describe a situation where a student's best friend was killed in an auto accident, and a peer will console this person.
4. Demonstrate this activity by role practicing this situation with a student.

GUIDELINES FOR ROLE PRACTICING

PURPOSE

The purpose of role practicing is to prepare students to function in real-life roles that relate to school situations by learning and practicing these roles. In this sense, role practicing, unlike role playing, is not playacting in make-believe roles.

Role practicing should increase the student's level of awareness about how to behave in specific peer related roles and provide the opportunity to practice good communication skills that are needed to properly execute them.

SIMULATION

Role practicing will simulate actual situations in a school setting so specific roles should not be foreign to the participants. However, students will have to think on their feet and react as if they were at school; therefore, they might feel awkward in this "on the spot" activity. To help students feel comfortable, the leader will demonstrate a role practicing activity with another student. Also, examples of role practicing activities are included in all the activities that use this training technique.

GUIDELINES

Specific guidelines for role practicing include the following:

1. Focus on the role that you need to be an effective leader, such as a counselor, motivator, facilitator, and so on.

2. Concentrate on the specific behavior needed to be an effective communicator. The emotion that you illustrate should match the situation, such as showing empathy in a counselor's role or excitement when congratulating a student for a job well done.

3. Visualize yourself at school and imagine what the situation would be like in terms of what the facility looks like and how you and the team member should relate to each other in this particular situation.

4. Select a school-related task that is appropriate for the specific role practicing activity. For example, a task that relates to learning how to say I-Feel Statements (to improve the communication process between two students) is a natural and easier one to simulate.

- Make a statement showing empathy for this person, and that you are available as a friend, to talk to him/her at any time.

- Change the subject and offer to do something fun with this person after school or on the weekend.

- If it feels right, put your arm around the person or hug him/her.

5. After this demonstration, get input from the students.

6. Ask students from each team to pair off with a teammate to role practice the same situation as illustrated previously.

7. Before role practicing, ask the students to close their eyes, visualize their feelings, and determine how they should relate to a grieving student.

8. Ask students to open their eyes and begin role practicing.

9. After two minutes, ask students to change roles.

10. Move from team to team, assist as needed.

11. Make sure that each pair has taken a turn.

Discussion (10 minutes)

Ask a student to volunteer to lead a critique by asking their teammates the following questions.

1. How did the consoling peer show empathy for the grieving peer?

2. What was the most effective thing that the consoling peer said to comfort the grieving peer?

3. What could you have said or done differently to comfort the peer?

Appreciation (5 minutes)

Ask each student to say one positive thing about what their partner did or said today.

Instructional Tips

1. Before demonstrating this activity, visualize yourself as a counselor consoling a student who has just lost his/her best friend.

   Think about how you will express your feelings through your tone of voice, saying the proper words, and conveying the appropriate actions. For example, you could approach a grieving student by saying: "John, I am really saddened to learn of Jim's death," and "I'm available at any time you need a friend to talk to." Or, ask the person if he/she would like to do something fun such as "Would you like to go to the Giants baseball game Friday night?"

2. It is best to begin this role practicing activity by having only two students role practice at a time with their teammates observing. This encourages everyone to role practice when their turn comes up. In the beginning when everyone pairs off at the same time, some students will just visit and not bother to role practice. Also, this provides an opportunity for students to observe the demonstration and critique accordingly.

3. An alternative activity could be the loss of a friend or relative by moving to another city. This situation is less traumatic and could be more appropriate for specific classroom settings. The teacher should use his/her good judgment and select the most appropriate activity for his/her class.

Anticipated Results

The students have learned how to role practice and they are prepared to use this technique in future activities.

ACTIVITY 2

LEARNING CONVERSATION SKILLS

Purpose

To understand how to start and conduct conversation with a stranger.

Skill Development

The student will learn how to:

✓ use techniques to begin a conversation
✓ ask open-ended questions
✓ practice good listening skills

Materials

• A chart illustrating open and closed questions
• A handout listing *Guidelines for Starting a Conversation*

- Paper pad and marking pens for recording brainstorming ideas

Introduction (2 minutes)

The leader will introduce this activity as follows:

1. Tell the students that today they will learn how to start a conversation with a stranger.

2. Inform them that they will learn some new techniques to make it easier for them to start and conduct a conversation.

3. Explain to them that it is easier to establish friendships and meet new people by engaging in a conversation.

Procedure (40 minutes)

The leader will conduct this activity as follows:

1. Have the students meet in their permanent teams.

2. Ask for volunteers from each team to act as a facilitator and a recorder.

3. Instruct the team to brainstorm typical approaches that individuals could use to start a conversation with someone new.

4. Remind the recorders to record these ideas on the paper pads.

5. Move from team to team and assist as needed.

6. At the conclusion of this activity, ask each team facilitator to share his/her list of ideas with the other teams.

7. Tell the recorder to list new ideas from the others' teams to their original list.

8. Role practice with a student to illustrate how to start a conversation.

9. Ask team members to observe and be prepared to critique this demonstration.

10. Begin the activity by introducing yourself by name and by asking the other person what his or her name is.

11. Ask a question like "What do you like to do in your spare time?"

12. Follow this person's answer with: "How did you get started with this activity?"

13. Pick up the theme of the person's last sentence and ask a related open-ended question, or tell this person that you share the same interest and converse accordingly. For example, if the student made a comment in his/her last sentence of "I got started in tennis by joining a tennis club," then the leader could ask, "What do you like most about belonging to a tennis club?"

Guidelines for Starting a Conversation

1. Open the conversation complimenting the other person's clothing, shoes, jewelry, or a physical feature such as a nice smile, pretty eyes, and so forth. Your tone of voice must be sincere and not sound phony. When complimenting a person for attractive physical features, the speaker must express his/her compliments in a very genuine and polite manner.

2. Smile and make good eye contact.

3. Find out what the other person's interest is by asking a question such as: "What do you like to do in your spare time?" Follow this question with an open-ended one such as: "How did you get started in (name the interest)?

4. Be a good listener and don't interrupt the other person. Listen carefully and pick up the theme of the last sentence and ask a related question, or tell this person that you share the same interest and converse accordingly.

5. Don't ask interview-type questions and avoid asking closed-ended questions that can be answered with a yes or no answer such as:

   • **Closed-ended:** "Do you like to play baseball?" **Answer:** Yes or No.

   • **Open-ended:** "Why do you like to play baseball?" **Answer:** "I like to play baseball with my friends."

   Related follow-up question: "When do you play baseball with your friends?"

6. Don't ask personal questions about things the other person hasn't talked about. Stick to the topic.

14. Critique this demonstration with the students.

15. Next, ask members from each team to pair off and practice this same activity.

16. At two-minute intervals, ask pairs to switch roles.

Discussion (if time permits, conduct a conversation)

Ask a team member to facilitate a discussion by asking the following questions:

1. How did you get to know your partner better?

2. Did you learn something new about your partner?

3. Did you share a similar interest with your partner?

Appreciation (omit)

Instructional Tips

1. Before moving into the role-practicing demonstration, pass out the handout "Guidelines for Starting a Conversation" and briefly cover key points. Students will implement these guidelines along with their original ideas.

2. Again, use this information to supplement the ideas that were generated from the brainstorming session.

3. Record examples of open-ended and closed-ended questions on a paper pad or blackboard, and refer to these examples during your explanation of how to begin a conversation.

Anticipated Results

The students understand how to start a conversation, and they feel comfortable conversing with a new friend.

ACTIVITY 3

LEARNING GOOD LISTENING SKILLS

Purpose

To understand the skills that are necessary to become a good listener.

Skill Development

The student will learn how to:

✓ use good eye contact

✓ listen carefully to the content and feelings behind the message

✓ acknowledge the speaker's message through reflective listening techniques

✓ practice asking good open-ended questions

Materials

Three Steps to Good Listening Skills handout

Introduction (2 minutes)

The leader will introduce this activity as follows:

1. Inform the students that today they will learn good listening skills.
2. Tell them that to conduct a warm and friendly conversation they must be good listeners.
3. Explain that they must understand the feeling and content of the message, and respond appropriately with a smile, nodding and asking open-ended questions.

Procedure (30 minutes)

The leader will conduct this activity as follows:

1. Ask the students to meet in their teams.
2. Refer to the handout listing good listening skills and explain the meaning of each skill.
3. Encourage questions and discussion from the students.
4. Ask for a student volunteer to pair off with you to demonstrate a role practicing activity.
5. Practice the role of the listener and the student will be the speaker.
6. Begin by asking the speaker to tell you about someone he/she admires a great deal.
7. Remind the student that this person can be a friend, relative, famous person, pet, or an object like a favorite possession.
8. Practice good listening skills and interject good open-ended questions to stimulate the conversation.
9. After this session, ask the students to identify the good listening skills that they observed during the activity.
10. Ask teammates to pair off and role practice this activity.
11. Tell the pairs to switch in three-minute intervals.
12. Move from team to team and assist accordingly.

Discussion (10 minutes)

Ask team leaders to volunteer to facilitate these discussions by asking the following questions:

1. Which good listening skills did your partner use?
2. How did it feel to be listened to? Explain.
3. How do you feel when people do not listen to you? Explain.
4. Was it difficult for you to be a good listener? Why?

Appreciation (5 minutes)

Ask each person to say one positive thing about what their partner did or said today.

Instructional Tips

1. The following three-step good listening process can be used as a handout and/or placed on the blackboard:

Three Steps to Good Listening Skills

Step 1: Focus on the speaker carefully through good eye contact. Listen keenly to the content and feeling behind the message.

Step 2: Use reflective listening by acknowledging that you understand the speaker's message by nodding, smiling, and saying something like, "I understand," "I agree," or "Good idea."

Step 3. Ask open-ended questions. Listen carefully to the theme of the last sentence spoken and then ask a related open-ended question.

---

2. During the role practicing demonstration, begin the conversation by making the following statement: "John, tell me about someone you admire a great deal." Continue this conversation by following the three-step process as illustrated above.

Anticipated Results

Students understand how to be a good listener. Students exhibit their ability to practice good listening skills during a conversation.

RECOGNIZING AND AVOIDING
POOR LISTENING HABITS

Purpose

To understand how to identify and avoid poor listening habits.

Skill Development

The students will learn how to:

✓ identify and recognize poor nonverbal and verbal listening skills
✓ counter poor listening skills with positive communication skills.

Materials

- *Poor Listening Skills* handout

Introduction (2 minutes)

The leader will introduce the activity as follows:

1. Explain to the students that today they will learn how to identify and avoid poor listening habits.
2. Inform them that poor listening habits prevent good conversation, and discourage friends from conversing with you.
3. Refer to the chart to provide a visual explanation of poor listening habits.

Procedure (30 minutes)

The leader will conduct this activity as follows:

1. Have the students meet in their teams. Pass out poor listening skills handout.
2. Refer the students to the charts listing poor listening skills, and ask them to brainstorm additional examples.
3. Ask a student to record these examples on a paper pad.
4. Remind the students they can use these examples and the examples on the chart during the role playing activity.
5. Ask for a student to pair off with you to role practice poor listening habits.
6. Ask the student to tell you about a favorite place to go on the weekend or for a vacation.

7. Respond to the student's response by demonstrating poor nonverbal and verbal listening skills (as illustrated on the chart).

8. Ask the students to critique the effectiveness of the listener.

9. After the critique ask the students to pair off with a teammate to role practice this same activity.

10. After two minutes, ask the pairs to switch roles.

11. Rotate from team to team and assist as needed.

Discussion (10 minutes)

Ask for volunteer student leaders to facilitate a discussion by asking the following questions:

1. Which poor listening habits bother you the most? Why?

2. How did you feel when your partner didn't listen to you? Explain.

3. Have you experienced times when a person didn't listen to you? Explain.

4. What did you learn from this exercise?

Appreciation (omit)

Instructional Tips

1. List the following nonverbal and verbal poor listening skills on a chart or handout to pass out to the students.

2. Refer to this material during your explanation of the topic.

Poor listening skills include nonverbal and verbal listening skills as follows:

Poor Listening Skills

NONVERBAL

- Not making eye contact by looking down or at someone else.
- Yawning and looking bored.
- Looking at your watch.
- Fidgeting or demonstrating a lack of interest.

(continued on next page)

Poor Listening Skills
(continued)

VERBAL

- Saying, "I only have two minutes of time to give you."
- Interrupting or changing the subject, an example could be: **Speaker:** "I'm really excited about my new project." **Listener:** "I can't wait to begin my vacation next Monday."
- The "me too syndrome" by drawing attention back to self. For example: **Speaker:** "I really feel bad about not reaching my weekly goals. **Listener:** "I met my weekly goals last week."
- The "advice syndrome" by telling the person what to do. An example could be: **Speaker:** "I wish Mr. Jones would help me with my math." **Listener:** "You don't need his help because you are smarter than he is."

Anticipated Results

Students understand how to identify and avoid poor listening habits. Students appreciate the importance of replacing poor listening habits with good listening habits.

ACTIVITY 5

LEARNING HOW TO OBSERVE OTHERS

Purpose

To understand how to observe and interpret the meaning of verbal and nonverbal patterns of communication.

Skill Development

The student will learn how to:

✓ observe and interpret the meaning of verbal and nonverbal patterns of communication

✓ check the accuracy of these interpretations through asking questions and reflective listening techniques

Materials

- *Verbal and Nonverbal Styles of Communication* handout
- A paper pad and marking pens for recording items

Introduction (30 minutes)

The leader will introduce this activity as follows:

1. Explain that today students will learn how to interpret the meaning of verbal and nonverbal behavior by carefully observing how people communicate with each other.

2. Tell them that the tone of voice, arm and hand gestures, facial expressions, and posture will indicate the mood of this person.

3. Explain that by understanding the feelings of another person, they will be better able to communicate with this person.

Procedure (30 minutes)

The leader will conduct this activity as follows:

1. Ask the students to meet in their teams.

2. Ask for volunteers from each team to act as facilitator and recorder.

3. Refer the teams to a chart/handout listing examples of typical verbal and nonverbal styles of communication to help familiarize them with these methods of communication.

4. Direct each team facilitator to lead a discussion by asking the following questions:

   - When your parents get home from work, how can you tell what kind of day they have had?
   - How can you tell what kind of mood your teacher is in?
   - How can you interpret the feelings of your peers?

5. Ask for the team recorder to copy the ideas generated from this discussion on a paper pad.

6. At the conclusion of this activity, ask the team facilitators to share their team's ideas with the other teams.

7. Ask a student to pair off with you to conduct a role practicing activity.

8. Describe a situation where a student has just been put down by another student because he failed to do a math problem correctly. A typical put-down could be "Joe, you are stupid, man."

9. Ask your partner to role practice his/her feeling for being put down.

10. Ask your partner to refer to the list of verbal and nonverbal mannerisms to select and act out the mannerisms that best describe his/her feelings.

11. Interpret his/her behavior by asking a question such as: "Mike are you angry about what happened?"

12. After Mike responds, follow up with another reflective listening technique to let him know you understand the content and feelings behind his message.

13. Ask teammates to pair off and practice this activity. After two minutes ask the partners to switch roles. Move from team to team and assist as needed.

Discussion (omit)

Appreciation (omit)

Instructional Tips

1. In preparation for activity 5, the leader should be adept at observing and interpreting nonverbal messages. Review of the following information will prepare the leader to better understand how to use these communication skills.

2. The nonverbal expressions of feelings or emotions can be very powerful. The body expresses what is in the mind. The observer must accurately interpret these nonverbal messages. Sound "translation" of nonverbal messages requires checking the accuracy of an interpretation of these messages. This is done through reflective listening techniques, whereby the observer asks the observed individual a question to validate the meaning of the nonverbal message. For example, if a person has a sneer on his face with his chest thrown out, ask the following question: "John, I notice that you have a definite sneer on your face. Are you angry about what happened?" After John responds, follow up with another reflective listening technique; use restating to let the speaker know that you understand the content and feelings behind his message. Refer to reflective listening techniques on page 78.

3. List the following verbal and nonverbal messages on a paper pad or the blackboard, or make up a handout of this information to pass out to the students.

Verbal and Nonverbal Styles of Communication

VERBAL MESSAGES:

Sounds: grunts, squeals, giggles, laughing

Speech tones: high- or low-pitched voice, shouting, quivering voice

Speech rate: fast, nervous, slow or hesitant, normal or confident

NONVERBAL MESSAGES:

Gesture: talking with the hands or arms, thumbs or fingers up or down, closed fist upraised, legs thrust out in a kicking motion

Posture: slouched shoulders, chest upraised, head on a desk, standing straight

Facial expressions: grin or smile, sneer or squint, puckered lips, furrowed forehead, raised eyebrows

---

4. To review the above messages, refer to each message and ask the students to give their interpretation of what each message means.

Anticipated Results

Students understand how to observe and interpret the meaning of verbal and nonverbal behavior. Students feel competent in interpreting the content and feelings of a specific behavior.

ACTIVITY 6

LEARNING HOW TO EMPATHIZE WITH OTHERS

Purpose

To understand how to listen from the heart in order to get in touch with another person's feelings.

Skill Development

The student will learn how to:

✓ employ reflective listening techniques to convey the understanding of a person's messages

✓ understand the feelings behind the words and actions of another person

Materials

- *Reflective Listening Techniques* handout
- *Words Illustrating Feelings and Emotions* chart

Introduction (5 minutes)

The leader will introduce this activity as follows:

1. Tell the students that today they will learn how to listen from their hearts so they can get in touch with another person's feelings.
2. Explain that as they hear what another person is saying, they must understand the feelings and actions behind the words.
3. Ask them to put themselves in the shoes of the other person, and try to experience what he/she is feeling.
4. Inform them that to empathize with another person, they must put aside their own concerns and become more interested in the other person.
5. State that they will learn reflective listening techniques, reporting back to the speaker his/her feelings and the content of his/her messages. They will also show this person that others care about him/her and understand the content of his/her message.

Procedure (30 minutes)

The leader will conduct this activity as follows:

1. Ask the students to meet in teams.
2. Refer each team back to their list of items in activity 5 and to the reflective listening techniques following this activity.
3. Ask for a student volunteer to do a role practicing activity with you.
4. Ask your partner to select the most disliked verbal or nonverbal behavior from their list of items from activity 5.
5. Before beginning the role practicing activity, review the reflective listening techniques and the list of feeling words following this activity.

6. Tell the students that they can use the list of feeling words as a guide to arrive at appropriate words to express their emotions during the role-practicing activity.

7. Begin the role-practicing activity by asking your partner an open-ended question such as: "Why does this (name the disliked behavior) offend you the most?"

8. As the student expresses his/her emotions, use reflective listening techniques to let him/her know you are in touch with his/her feelings and understand the message.

9. After two minutes of conversation ask the observing students to identify and describe examples of reflective listening techniques used by the leader.

10. Next, ask the students to select a verbal or nonverbal style of communication that they dislike and then pair off with a teammate to role practice this same activity.

11. After two minutes, ask the partners to change roles.

12. Move from team to team and assist as needed.

Discussion (10 minutes)

Ask a student leader to facilitate this discussion by asking the following questions:

1. Which reflective listening techniques did your partner use?

2. How did your partner show that he/she cared for your feelings?

3. What did you learn from this activity?

Appreciation (5 minutes)

Ask each person within each team to say one thing that is positive about what their partner did or said today.

Instructional Tips

1. During the reflective listening activity, use the handout to illustrate the meaning of each of the following techniques: *clarifying, restating, summarizing, validating,* and *encouraging.* Refer to the question or statement at the end of each reflective listening technique listed on the handout.

2. To help the students learn how to empathize or get in touch with another person's feelings, review the list of feeling words that describes various emotions. Relate these emotions to situations that arise during the role-practicing activity.

   List these feeling words on a paper pad or make up a handout to pass out to the students.

REFLECTIVE LISTENING TECHNIQUES

Reflective listening is acknowledging that you understand the speaker's message and the feelings behind the message by giving verbal and nonverbal feedback. Don't interrupt the speaker, but reflect back in your own words that you understand the content and feelings of the speaker's message. Reflective listening includes the following techniques:

CLARIFYING

Ask open-ended questions to get a clear understanding or interpretation of what is said. An example would be to ask the following question: "Help me understand the situation. What was the problem between the two of you?"

RESTATING

Restate the speaker's message in your own words to let the speaker know that you understand the content and feelings behind the message. A sample statement would be: "I hear you saying that you feel your teacher is impatient with you." Focus your statement on the basic ideas and facts of the speaker's message.

SUMMARIZING

Summarize the speaker's message to review and pull together important ideas and facts by restating the major ideas or facts to establish a basis for further conversation. An example of summarizing would be: "So you've been to see both teachers and one of them won't sign your contract."

VALIDATING

Validating the speaker's message acknowledges the positive meaning of the statement. A sample statement might be, "Thanks for caring about us."

ENCOURAGING

Encouraging the speaker to continue talking by taking an interest in what he/she is saying. An example would be: "Tell me more about the situation."

Words Illustrating Feelings and Emotions

Frustrated—anxious, worried, nervous, uptight, concerned

Calm—composed, serene, cool, tranquil, steady

Afraid—frightened, terrified, scared, fearful, intimidated

Angry—mad, offended, furious, displeased, annoyed

Happy—elated, glad, delighted, cheerful, merry

Sad—unhappy, sorrowful, dejected, miserable, gloomy

Anticipated Results

Students understand how to get in touch with feelings that are representative of the words and actions of others. Students are competent in conveying their messages through reflective listening techniques.

ACTIVITY 7

WELCOMING A NEW STUDENT

Purpose

To make a new student feel welcome and comfortable in class.

Skill Development

The student will learn how to:

- use positive communication skills to welcome a new student to class

Materials

- A paper pad
- Marking pens

Introduction (2 minutes)

The leader will introduce this activity as follows:

1. Tell the students that today they will learn how to welcome a new student to class.

2. Explain to them that they will use the positive communications skills that they have been learning and practicing to welcome new students such as: *conversation, listening, observing,* and *empathy* skills.

Procedure (35 minutes)

The leader will conduct this activity as follows:

1. Direct the students to meet in their permanent teams.

2. Begin by sharing your own experiences or feelings as a student or a person in a new setting.

3. Ask for volunteers from each team to act as a facilitator and a recorder.

4. Instruct the facilitators to lead a team discussion about what it feels like to be a new person in a new setting.

5. After five minutes of discussion ask team facilitators to lead a brainstorming session. Ask teams to arrive at positive and caring things they can do to make a new student feel comfortable in class.

6. Have the recorder list these items on the paper pad.

7. At the conclusion of this activity ask each team facilitator to share his/her list with the other teams.

8. From these various lists instruct the students to prioritize and compile one list of items.

9. Ask for a volunteer from each team to participate on a welcoming committee. Use the list of items as guidelines for welcoming a new student to school.

Discussion (omit)

Appreciation (omit)

Instructional Tips

1. If time permits, ask a student to practice the role of a new student in class. Have the welcoming committee welcome this new student to class.

2. If time has elapsed, conduct this activity during the next class period.

Anticipated Results

Students understand how to make a new student feel comfortable in class. Students feel competent in exercising this process.

LEARNING HOW TO MAKE I-FEEL STATEMENTS

Purpose

To understand how to replace negative "You" statements with positive "I" statements.

Skill Development

The student will:

✓ understand the meaning of I-Feel statements and "you" statements

✓ learn how to communicate his/her feelings by arriving at I-messages to replace "you" messages

Materials

- *"I" and "You" Messages* handout
- *"I" and "You" Messages* worksheet
- *Words Illustrating Feelings and Emotions* handout (from activity 6)

Introduction (5 minutes)

The leader will introduce this activity as follows:

1. Tell the students that today they will learn how to communicate their feelings through "I-Feel" statements.

2. Explain that they are responsible for letting their peers and friends know how their behavior affects them.

3. Inform them that it is typical to put the other person down or offend another person with a "You" statement.

4. Refer to the handout and explain what a "You" message is.

5. Explain that by using direct, positive I-messages, you can express your feelings without offending others.

6. Refer to the handout of I-Feel statements.

Procedure (30 minutes)

The leader will conduct this activity as follows:

1. Ask the students to meet in their teams.

2. Seat the team around a table or have students put their desks in a cluster.

3. Pass out the "I" and "You" message handouts and review the material.

4. Pass out a list of feeling words and the "I" and "You" message worksheets to all students. See worksheet at end of activity.

5. Ask teammates to work in pairs to complete the worksheets.

6. Refer to situation 1 on the worksheet and review the sample "you" and "I" messages to give the student an understanding of how to complete the other situations.

   • Ask the pairs to complete the "you" and "I" message situations 2 to 6 on the worksheet.

   • Remind the students to use words from the "feeling words" list to express their feelings appropriately.

   • Tell them that you will help them with the definitions of these words as needed.

Discussion (omit)

Appreciation (omit)

Instructional Tips

1. When referring to the I-message handout, illustrate how an I-message consists of three parts.

2. Tell the students to use their own words when saying an I-message rather than trying to memorize and say three parts of speech (which sometimes becomes cumbersome or confusing).

3. Remind the students to begin a "You" message with "you" as illustrated in the handout.

Anticipated Results

Students understand how to arrive at I-Feel messages. Students recognize the importance of replacing "you" messages with I-Feel messages. Students feel capable of arriving at and using an I-message in the proper context.

"I" AND "YOU" MESSAGES

© 1995 by The Center for Applied Research in Education

POSITIVE CONFRONTATION

When confronting a team member about a communication problem, you should be assertive and speak in terms of how this person's action affects you on a personal level (use "I" messages). Don't confront a team member in an aggressive manner that puts this person "down" or attempts to make him/her look stupid by using "you" messages.

"I" MESSAGES

An "I" message has three parts:

    (1) the feeling that results from the other person's behavior

    (2) the behavior that is exhibited by the other person

    (3) the tangible effect as a result of this behavior

When using an "I" message, you should use your own choice of words and think in terms of how this behavior affects you on a personal level rather than putting the blame for the behavior on the other person. *Examples of "I" messages are as follows:*

Feeling:	I feel great
Behavior:	When you help me with my algebra
Tangible Effect:	Because I am able to complete my assignment correctly
Feeling:	I feel frustrated
Behavior:	When you interrupt me
Tangible Effect:	Because I have some important information to share with you

The following material describes "I" message behavior:

Actions:	Calm manner, controlled movements, good eye contact

© 1995 by The Center for Applied Research in Education

Words: I'm angry
Please don't interrupt me
Because I have some good news to tell you

Feelings: Confident, responsible, and sensitive to others' feelings

"YOU" MESSAGES

Most people use blaming or "you" messages to convey their feelings when they are mad or frustrated. An aggressive "you" message offends the other person or makes him/her feel stupid. "You" messages usually take the following form:

Ordering: "You will not go to the concert."

Warning: "You had better improve your school attendance or you will have to stay after school to make up time."

Judging: "That was a stupid thing for you to do."

Name Calling: "You stupid jerk."

An example of a "You" message is:

"You jerk, stop interrupting me or I won't talk to you anymore."

The following describes aggressive "you" message behavior:

Actions: Physical contact, nasty stares, angry

Words: If you interrupt me one more time, I'm leaving because you are a very inconsiderate person.

Feelings: Angry, selfish, insecure

"I" AND "YOU" MESSAGES WORK SHEET

Directions: Print an "I" and a "You" message for each situation. The first is completed for you.

SITUATION	"YOU" MESSAGE	"I" MESSAGE
1. A person interrupts you.	1. You jerk! Shut-up or I won't talk to you anymore.	1. I'm angry when you call me names because I want to be treated with respect.
2. A friend ignores you.	2. _____	2. _____
3. A friend borrows money and does not pay it back.	3. _____	3. _____
4. A peer teases you a lot in front of others.	4. _____	4. _____
5. A peer takes something of yours without asking. ____	5. _____	5. _____
6. A friend gossips about you and other friends. _____	6. _____	6. _____

ACTIVITY 9

LEARNING HOW TO SAY "I-FEEL" STATEMENTS

Purpose

To understand how to say an I-Feel statement in a direct and caring way.

Skill Development

The student will learn how to:

✓ understand the importance of using I-messages instead of "you" messages

✓ correctly say the three-part I-feel message

✓ be assertive and express his/her true feelings in a direct and caring way

Materials

"I" and "You" Messages handout from activity 8

Introduction (2 minutes)

The leader will introduce this activity as follows:

1. Tell the students that today they will learn how to say I-Feel statements.
2. Explain that they will use an I-message to express their feelings about how another person is treating them.
3. State that they will use I-messages in a firm but caring way rather than saying "you" messages which offend other people.

Procedure (30 minutes)

The leader will conduct this activity as follows:

1. Ask the students to meet in their teams.
2. Leader pairs off with a student to role practice an activity.
3. Ask the students to observe and critique this demonstration.
4. Ask your partner to interrupt, give advice, and change the subject during this role-practicing discussion.

5. Begin by discussing where you plan to go for a vacation. Try to be descriptive and give details.

6. Respond by illustrating an assertive I-message and for comparison, an aggressive "you" message.

7. Ask the students to give their impressions of the two illustrations.

8. Refer the students to the sample illustration to use as a guide during the role practicing activity.

9. Ask the teammates to pair off and role practice this same activity.

10. Move from team to team and assist as needed.

Discussion (10 minutes)

Ask a volunteer from each team to facilitate a discussion by asking the following questions:

1. What was difficult about using an I-Feel message?

2. How can you simplify using an I-Feel message?

3. How can you use I-Feel messages to improve your communications with friends or family members?

4. Do your friends or family use "you" or "I-Feel" statements?

Appreciation (omit)

Instructional Tips

1. When pairing off with a student to role practice this activity, use the following "I" and "You" messages as guidelines. In this situation, your partner constantly interrupts you while you are talking.

   - **"I" Message:** "John, I feel frustrated

     when you interrupt me

     because I want to tell you about my vacation."

   - **"You" Message:** "You are so rude—

     stop interrupting me,

     you jerk."

2. During the critique ask the students to describe the kind of "you" messages that you used. Then ask them to describe the different emotions of your partner as he/she responded to the "I" and "you" messages.

Anticipated Results

Students understand how to use I-Feel statements in a direct and caring way. Students feel competent in saying an I-message to express their true feelings.

ACTIVITY 10

LEARNING TO BECOME ASSERTIVE

Purpose

To understand how to resist peer pressure by being assertive and using I-messages rather than being aggressive and using "you" messages.

Skill Development

The student will learn how to:

- resist negative peer pressure through assertive I-messages
- use alternative ways for resisting negative peer pressure without offending a peer or friend

Materials

- *Resisting Peer Pressure* handout
- *Types of Behavior for Resisting Peer Pressure* handout
- Paper pads and marking pens for recording items

Introduction (3 minutes)

The leader will introduce this activity as follows:

1. Explain that today students will learn to resist negative peer pressure through assertive behavior.
2. Tell them they will use assertive behavior to stand up for their rights and to state their own beliefs and opinions. In addition, they will refrain from using aggressive behavior like bullying or putting down others.
3. Inform them that in today's activity they will practice assertive behavior by using "I" messages.

Procedure (40 minutes)

1. Ask students to meet in teams.
2. Ask for volunteers to act as facilitators and recorders for each team.
3. Begin by asking each team to define and describe what negative peer pressure means to them.
4. Ask the recorder to print these definitions on their paper pads.
5. Ask the team facilitators to brainstorm typical situations where students are influenced by peer pressure.
6. Tell the recorders to print these items on their paper pads.
7. After five minutes of brainstorming, ask each team to select a topic from their list. Have team members discuss approaches they can use to resist this peer pressure situation.
8. Pass out the two handouts on resisting peer pressure.
9. Ask teams to compare these approaches with their own thoughts of how to resist negative peer pressure.
10. Leader pairs off with a student and role practices the situation that was selected by the student's team.
11. Ask your partner to approach you with the idea of influencing you to participate in this activity.
12. Respond by using an assertive statement such as: "No (state the name of a partner) I can't do (specify the activity) because (say an I-message indicating why you can't participate in this activity).
13. Next, respond by demonstrating an aggressive "you" message.
14. Ask for two students from each team to refer to their selected situation and role practice for the assertive "I" and "you" message techniques.
15. At the conclusion of this activity ask each team to critique their demonstration and note the differences for the "I" and "you" message techniques.
16. If time permits, ask the other students to pair off and role practice their selected situations.

Discussion (omit)

Instructional Tips

1. Before role practicing this activity ask each team to compare their approaches with the illustrations for resisting peer pressure and arrive at what they believe to be the best approach.
2. Explain how passive and passive-aggressive behavior relates to saying "yes" to participating in negative peer-pressure situations. Refer to the handout for examples.

Anticipated Results

Students understand how to say "no" to negative peer pressure—they are strong enough to stand up for their beliefs and have the ability to use an assertive I-message technique.

RESISTING PEER PRESSURE

GUIDELINES

Use the following guidelines to determine what to do or say when resisting negative peer pressure:

- Use an assertive "I" message to take responsibility for your own feelings and actions.

- Do not use an aggressive "you" message to offend your peers when resisting peer pressure. Instead, just walk away from the situation with dignity and grace.

- Suggest positive alternative behavior to replace negative behavior or peer pressure.

- Take a positive course of action that you believe is right, be strong, and stand by your decision.

EXAMPLES OF HOW TO RESIST NEGATIVE PEER PRESSURE

Situation 1: Your friends invite you to drink beer on Saturday night. You don't want to participate. What will you say or do?

"Kim, I can't drink beer because I promised my dad that I would not drink beer. Let's go to the movies."

Situation 2: Your peers decide to beat up a rival gang member and you don't want to get involved in this fight. What will you say or do?

"Jose, I don't have anything against Mario. I'm not going to hurt him because I don't want to end up in Juvie (Juvenile Hall)."

Situation 3: Your friends are planning to wear earrings and get a "mowhawk" hair cut. You don't feel comfortable looking like that. What will you say or do?

"John, I don't want to get a "mowhawk." "Let's get a flat-top instead because it looks better."

Situation 4: Your friends ask you to go "drag racing" with thim. You are afraid of getting into a dangerous accident. What will you say or do?

"Robin, I'm not going drag racing. I don't want to end up in the hospital."

TYPES OF BEHAVIOR
FOR RESISTING PEER PRESSURE

ASSERTIVE BEHAVIOR:

An assertive person stands up for his/her beliefs and values, and is not influenced by peer pressure to do something he/she believes is not the right thing to do.

Actions: Calm manner, positive response, under control, firm and definite

Feelings: Confident, secure, sensitive

Typical Assertive Statement: "I can't do this because I don't think it is the right thing to do and I don't want to get into trouble."

AGGRESSIVE BEHAVIOR:

An aggressive person stands up for her/his own beliefs and values, but resists peer pressure by threatning others through physical contact, put-down messages, negative stares and gestures.

Actions: Agitated, boistrous, angry

Feelings: Insensitive, insecure, selfish

Typical Aggressive Statement: "You idiot! You must think I'm stupid to do something like that."

PASSIVE BEHAVIOR:

A passive person does not stand up for his/her own beliefs and values and gives in to the demands of peer pressure.

Actions: Meek, timid, weak voice, poor posture

Feelings: Insecure, afraid, nervous

Typical Statement: "Yeh I'll do it." "OK you win."

PASSIVE-AGGRESSIVE BEHAVIOR:

A passive-aggressive person seems to agree to the demands of a peer; agreeing to do the deed, but disguising feelings that are expressed in different ways; trying to make the other person feel guilty for applying peer pressure.
mean something else, hide feelings that come out in different ways, and try to make the other person feel guilty about the request.

Actions: Sly, sarcastic, high/low voice, grin/sneer

Feelings: Insecure, selfish, fearful, repressed anger

Typical Statement: "Yeh, I'll do it, but I'll probably get into trouble with my parents because of you, but lets do it anyway."

PROBLEM SOLVING

INTRODUCTION

Most at-risk students have difficulty coping with school, family, and peer related problems. Section III teaches students the critical thinking skills needed to successfully cope with these problems. However, to properly execute critical thinking skills, students must learn positive communication skills. (Section II on Communication should be covered to prepare for this section.) For example, to resolve a conflict or act as a peer helper students must be able to:

- use good listening skills and ask good open-ended questions
- utilize reflective listening techniques
- say positive I-messages

The learning of critical thinking skills to complement positive communication skills augments the Discipline Prevention Program. For example, through the application of good communication and critical-thinking skills, students can resolve personal conflicts and avoid severe discipline problems in the classroom. Activity 7 explains how to use the critical thinking process to solve a typical discipline problem in the classroom.

Before describing how to use the critical thinking process to solve discipline problems, it is important for the reader to gain an understanding of what it encompasses. The following steps provide a general explanation of the critical thinking process. Specific examples of real-life applications of this process will follow the explanation of the *Six-Step Critical Thinking Process.*

Six-Step Critical Thinking Process

1. *Define and Clarify*

    The first step is to arrive at a definition of:
    - a problem through a problem-solving activity
    - a situation through a decision-making activity
    - a conflict through a conflict-resolution activity

    (continued on next page)

Six-Step Critical Thinking Process
(continued)

- a project or task through a school or community service project

- a subject or topic through a research report activity

It is necessary to clarify a definition to be sure it is absolutely clear and concise. Most problems, situations, or conflicts can be defined and clarified by asking open-ended questions and getting satisfactory answers.

2. *Gather and Review*

The next step is to gather and review alternative ways or solutions to solve a problem, resolve a conflict, or select choices for making a decision. Brainstorming and asking open-ended questions are used to gather this information.

Note: When completing steps 1 and 2 to complete a research report and conduct a community service project, additional facts and information are needed via:

- instructional materials

- library resources

- expertise from an expert in the field

This information is reviewed to determine which categories to place data in for a research report, and which tasks are needed to conduct a service project. (See activities 11 and 17 for specific examples.)

3. *Analyze and Evaluate*

The next step is to weigh the pros and cons of each alternative solution or the negative and positive consequences of each choice or decision. When weighing this information think in terms of the impact the decision will have on self and others.

By analyzing and evaluating the materials for a research report, the student will have the necessary information to understand how to cope with problems and make tough decisions relating to drugs, sex, or peer problems. Through analyzing and evaluating the facts and information needed to conduct a community service project, students will have the necessary information to prioritize and place tasks in sequential order by completion dates. Furthermore, they will have the

(continued on next page)

Six-Step Critical Thinking Process
(continued)

data needed for designing an action plan as a guide to implementing the project.

4. *Make a Decision*

   The next step is to decide which alternative solution or choice would be the best, or in the case of a conflict among peers, making a decision where both parties can win. When working on a community service project, students decide which tasks each person is responsible for. When conducting a research report, students will review their analysis and evaluation per step 3, and decide on the best choice.

5. *Implement the Decision*

   The first step towards implementing a decision is to record the decision as a goal on the action plan provided. Next, identify the steps needed to implement the decision, such as:

   - Who will implement the action plan?

   - What will they need to do?

   - How will they do it?

   - When and where will this action take place?

   Steps 3 and 4 identify barriers that could deter these steps and provide strategies for dealing with them. Step 5 sets a deadline for implementing the decision. Refer to *Steps for Implementing a Decision* found in activity 2.

   To implement a service project, an action plan must include:

   - the tasks to be completed

   - the assigned students to do the tasks

   - the time lines and due dates for completing each task

6. *Follow-up and Evaluation of an Action Plan*

   The student's progress is checked at a review meeting and a decision is made to stay on course or to make revisions to the action plan. Periodic follow-ups should take place until it is certain that the student is following a course of action that works.

It is important students understand how to implement this six-step process. To provide the focus and concentration needed to learn critical thinking steps, steps are taught sequentially during separate class periods or activities as follows:

- define and clarify a problem in activity 1

- arrive at alternative solutions and weigh the pros and cons of each solution in activity 2

- make and implement a decision in activity 3

During the teaching of activities 1, 2, and 3, the teacher or counselor must emphasize the purpose of each critical thinking step so students understand why each step is necessary to conduct the critical thinking process.

Activity 1 is designed to identify a discipline problem in the classroom. Through a brainstorming activity, students select "verbally abusing each other through put-down statements" as their major discipline problem. Students trace this discipline problem through activities 1, 2, and 3, and they use the critical thinking process to:

- define and clarify why students verbally abuse each other

- arrive at alternative solutions for solving the problem such as:

  ✓ using build-up statements to replace put-down statements

  ✓ using positive I-messages to confront a classmate rather than negative "you" statements

  ✓ abiding by the Behavioral Code for expected behavior in the classroom

- weigh the pros and cons of each solution

- decide upon the best solution or solutions

- design and implement an action plan

- conduct a follow-up review meeting to check each student's progress in his/her execution of the action plan

By choosing a discipline problem that is relevant to them, students are able to relate the critical thinking process to a typical problem they face in the classroom or on school grounds. This approach should help the students learn how to use this process and prepare them for solving future peer- or school-related discipline problems.

In activities 4, 5, and 6, student support teams apply the six steps simultaneously as follows:

- Team members help a teammate solve a personal problem.

- A team member solves his/her own personal problem.

- A team member acts as a peer coach to help a teammate solve his/her personal problem.

These activities provide students with an opportunity to practice and learn the critical-thinking steps. The remaining activities in Section III are used as a vehicle to teach students the critical thinking process. They are designed to teach students how to:

- resolve or mediate a personal conflict
- complete a cooperative research report
- conduct a community or school service project

Situations dealing with school or peer problems can evolve into discipline problems easily. For instance, major discipline problems are occurring on today's school campuses because of violence resulting from:

- guns in school
- gang activity
- drug use and drug dealing on school grounds

Consequently, conflict can result and students and teachers are sometimes verbally and physically abused. In this instance, severe discipline problems occur, and students, teachers, counselors, and administrators must have the means to cope with or solve these problems successfully. Through this guide, students, teachers, and counselors will learn how to apply the six-step critical thinking process to resolve a personal conflict between two students. It should be the role of the teacher and counselor to train students to resolve their own conflicts; this is the most meaningful approach. Also, these trained student leaders can conduct classroom or school meetings to deal with serious discipline problems in the classroom or on school grounds. For example, when dealing with a serious discipline problem such as carrying a gun to school, a student leader or leaders can conduct a meeting through a school assembly to:

- define and clarify why this is a serious problem
- arrive at ways to solve the problem such as:
  - ✓ inspect students on school grounds
  - ✓ hire security guards to patrol school grounds
  - ✓ suspend or expel students from school
  - ✓ get parental support to keep children from carrying guns to school
  - ✓ use positive peer pressure through student leaders and peer support teams to control this problem
- weigh the pros and cons of each solution
- decide upon the best solution or solutions
- design and implement an action plan to execute the decision
- conduct a follow-up review meeting to check the progress of the action plan

Thus, through this six-step process students can devise their own system for handling discipline problems in the classroom or on school grounds.

Alcohol and drug abuse is also spreading throughout many schools in America, resulting in discipline problems. To combat this problem, students complete a cooperative research report in activities 10 to 14 to:

- define and clarify the problems resulting from the use of alcohol and other drugs

- gather and review facts and information about alcohol and other drugs

- analyze and evaluate the facts and information covering alcohol and other drugs

- have the option to make a decision to abstain from alcohol or drug use

- design and execute an action plan to execute this decision

- conduct a follow-up review meeting to check each student's progress and decide whether to stay on course or make revisions in the plan.

Students who have discipline problems in school because of using alcohol or other drugs are encouraged to change their behavior through this six-step process. Refer to activity 14 for a specific action plan for dealing with drug problems.

As a follow-up to the cooperative research report, students are to conduct a drug prevention school service project. In their report, they are to design a program that prevents drug use and associated discipline problems from occurring on school grounds. Refer to activities 15 to 19 for more information.

Cooperative Learning

This guide recommends the use of cooperative learning instruction techniques to complement Student Support Teams because teammates support each other to reach their educational goals.

The *Student Achievement Division (STAD) Cooperative Learning* technique is recommended for study teams in regular or self-contained classrooms. The teacher provides instruction and assigns students a lesson to complete. Teammates assist each other until every member of the team understands the instructional material and has completed the assignment successfully. They may work in pairs or in triads to ask questions, compare answers, provide tutoring, and quiz each other before taking a test. Under the teacher's guidance they are to use instructional aides and assist each other. Through this cooperative process, students read, discuss, and manipulate instructional materials that take into account visual, audio, and action-oriented learning styles. This approach enhances the learning process.

However, students must pass tests on their own without any help from teammates. A student's test score is compared with his/her past test scores and points are awarded for meeting or improving on a previous test. These points are added to a team score. When teams meet specific performance criteria, they can earn certificates or other awards deemed appropriate for the situation.

The teacher moves from team to team to facilitate this cooperative learning process. It takes from three to five class periods to complete an assignment and take tests.

In this guide, the "jigsaw cooperative learning method" is used to complete a cooperative research report on alcohol and drug abuse. This instructional process is described in detail in activities 10 to 14. This technique works well in a self-contained individualized instructional program since students with like ability can form teams to study the same subject. This cooperative learning technique works well with the success oriented instructional process described in Section I.

See reference for more information: Robert E. Slavin, *Using Student Team Learning,* Third Edition.

ACTIVITY 1

DEFINING AND CLARIFYING A PROBLEM

STEP 1 OF THE CRITICAL THINKING PROCESS

Purpose

To understand how to define and clarify a problem.

Skill Development

The student will learn how to:

✓ define and clarify a problem

✓ practice brainstorming and discussion techniques

✓ practice using good open-ended questions and good listening skills

Materials

- *Six-Step Critical Thinking Process* handout
- *Six-Step Problem Solving Process* handout
- Paper pads and marking pens for recording brainstorming items

Introduction (2 minutes)

The leader will introduce this activity as follows:

1. Tell the students that today they begin learning critical thinking skills.
2. Inform them to focus on the first step of this process—how to define and clarify a problem.
3. Explain why it is important to define and clarify a problem as a first step of the critical thinking process.
4. Refer to the handout and remind them that these problem solving and decision making skills will help them cope with personal problems.

Procedure (30 minutes)

The leader will conduct this activity as follows:

1. Ask the students to meet in their teams.
2. Ask for volunteers to lead a brainstorming session to arrive at typical discipline problems that students have in the classroom or on the school grounds

relating to academics, peer associations, and drug use. (**Note:** Ask the students to discuss these issues on a general basis and do not get personal.)

3. Ask for a volunteer from each team to record these items on a paper pad.

4. After brainstorming for five minutes, ask each team to offer a consensus on which problem area is the most popular or thought provoking.

5. Move from team to team to assist as needed.

6. Ask team facilitators to lead a discussion with team members, sharing their own experiences plus those that they have heard about in their teams' problem areas.

7. Remind the team facilitators to ask open-ended questions and use good listening skills.

8. After each team member has shared his/her experience, ask each team to summarize the main ideas and arrive at a definition of their problems. (See illustration in *Instructional Tips.*)

9. Pass out Six-Step Problem Solving handout and ask students to record their definitions on Step 1.

10. To clarify their definitions, ask teams to discuss their definitions to be sure they are is comprehensive enough to define the specifics of their problems.

11. Move from team to team to help facilitate this process.

12. Reproduce additional copies of the Six-Step Problem Solving handouts as this handout will be used in other problem solving activities.

Discussion (omit)

Appreciation (omit)

Instructional Tips

1. In preparation for this activity record the six-step critical thinking process on a paper pad, make a permanent chart, or distribute the handout. Briefly explain how students can use this process to solve typical teen problems.

2. Before the discussion activity, remind students about the importance of observing the confidentiality ground rule.

3. Before summarizing the main ideas, demonstrate to the class how to pull the main ideas from several statements to arrive at one definition. After summarizing their main ideas they arrive at the following definition: Students feel hurt and angry when classmates verbally abuse them in classroom or on school grounds. Ask students to record their definitions on Step 1 of the Six Step Problem Solving Process handout.

4. For illustration purposes, a team in this activity selected students verbally abusing each other with "put-down statements" as their discipline problem.

Anticipated Results

Students understand how to define and clarify a problem area by defining a typical discipline problem that affects them on a personal level.

SIX-STEP CRITICAL THINKING PROCESS

1. *Define and Clarify*

   The first step is to arrive at a definition of:

   - a problem through a problem solving activity
   - a situation through a decision-making activity
   - a conflict through a conflict-resolution activity
   - a project or task through a school or community service project
   - a subject or topic through a research report activity

   It is necessary to clarify a definition to be sure it is absolutely clear and concise. Most problems, situations, or conflicts can be defined and clarified by asking open-ended questions and getting satisfactory answers.

2. *Gather and Review*

   The next step is to gather and review alternative ways or solutions to solve a problem, resolve a conflict, or select choices for making a decision. Brainstorming and asking open-ended questions are used to gather this information.

   Note: When completing steps 1 and 2 to complete a research report and conduct a community service project, additional facts and information are needed via:

   - instructional materials
   - library resources
   - expertise from an expert in the field

   This information is reviewed to determine which categories to place data in for a research report, and which tasks are needed to conduct a service project.

3. *Analyze and Evaluate*

   The next step is to weigh the pros and cons of each alternative solution, or the negative and positive consequences of each choice or decision. When weighing this information, think in terms of the impact the decision will have on oneself and others.

   By analyzing and evaluating the materials for a research report, the student will have the necessary information to understand how to cope with problems and make tough decisions relating to drugs, sex, or peer problems.

(continued on next page)

Through analyzing and evaluating the facts and information needed to conduct a community service project, students will have the necessary information to prioritize and place tasks into sequential order by completion dates, and will have the data needed for designing an action plan for implementing the project.

4. *Make a Decision*

The next step is to decide which alternative solution or choice would be the best, or, in the case of a conflict among peers, making a decision whereby both parties can win. When working on a community service project, students decide which tasks each person is responsible for, and when conducting a research report, students will review their analysis and evaluation per step 3, and decide on the best choice.

5. *Implement the Decision*

The first step towards implementing a decision is to record the decision as a goal on the action plan. Next, identify the steps needed to implement the decision, such as:

- who will implement the action plan

- what they will need to do

- how will they do it

- when and where will this action take place

Steps 3 and 4 identify barriers that could deter these steps and provide strategies for dealing with them. Step 5 sets a deadline for implementing the decision. Refer to *Steps for Implementing a Decision* handout.

To implement a service project, an action plan includes:

- the tasks to be completed

- the assigned students who will perform the tasks

- the time lines and due dates for task completion

6. *Follow-Up and Evaluation of an Action Plan*

The student's progress is checked at a review meeting and a decision is made to stay on course or to make revisions in the action plan. Periodic follow-ups should take place until it is certain that the student is following a course of action that is working.

SIX-STEP PROBLEM SOLVING PROCESS HANDOUT

STEPS

1. Define and clarify the problem.

   * _____

   _____

   _____

2. Select alternative solutions to solve this problem.

   * _____

   * _____

   * _____

   * _____

   * _____

   * _____

3. Weigh the pros and cons of each alternative solution in terms of negative and positive consequences.

   POSITIVE   *NEGATIVE*

   * _____   * _____

   * _____   * _____

   * _____   * _____

   * _____   * _____

   * _____   * _____

   * _____   * _____

4. Decide on the best alternative solution or solutions.

   * _____

   _____

5. Implement the decision (refer to *Steps for Implementing a Decision* handout).

6. Follow up to evaluate the results of the above-mentioned handout. (Refer to step 6).

ACTIVITY 2

ARRIVING AT AND EVALUATING AN ALTERNATIVE SOLUTION

STEPS 2 AND 3 OF THE CRITICAL THINKING PROCESS

Purpose

To understand how to arrive at and evaluate alternative solutions that are necessary steps for solving a problem.

Skill Development

The student will:

✓ learn how to arrive at and evaluate alternative solutions

✓ practice brainstorming, discussion, and positive communication skills

Materials

- The *Six-Step Critical Thinking Process* handout (from activity 1)
- Paper pads and marking pens for recording brainstorming items
- *Six-Step Problem Solving Process* handout (from activity 1)
- *Steps for Implementing a Decision* handout

Introduction (3 minutes)

The leader will introduce the activity as follows:

1. Inform the students that today they will cover steps 2 and 3 of the critical-thinking process.
2. Refer to these steps on the chart handout.
3. Explain why steps 2 and 3 are important to the critical thinking process.
4. Tell them they will brainstorm alternative solutions for solving the problems teams identified in activity 1. They will weigh the pros and cons of each solution.

Procedure

The leader will conduct this activity as follows:

1. Ask the students to meet in their teams.
2. Ask the same team facilitators to continue with this activity.
3. Tell each facilitator to refer to their team's definition of the agreed-upon problem area.
4. Give team members an opportunity to ask questions or add information to further clarify the problem area.
5. Monitor the teams and keep this discussion to a five-minute time limit.
6. Inform the facilitators to lead a brainstorming session to arrive at alternative solutions for solving the problems the teams selected in activity 1.
7. Tell the recorder to document all solutions for each problem on the paper pad.
8. Pass out the problem solving forms and ask students to copy items down on them. Step 2 of the Six-Step form.
9. When the list of alternative solutions is complete, ask team leaders to move to step 3 and review the pros and cons of each solution.
10. To get this process started, role practice with a team to list the pros and cons of an alternative solution.
11. Ask team leaders to continue this process.
12. Remind recorders to write the pros and cons for each solution on their paper pads. Ask team members to record pros and cons on Step 3 of their problem solving forms.

Discussion (omit)

Appreciation (omit)

Instructional Tips

1. After clarifying the definition of their team's problem, ask students to record this definition on step 1 of their problem-solving form.
2. There are six spaces provided to record the pros and cons of the six alternative solutions. If the recorders need more space, they can use the back of the Six-Step Problem Solving Process handout.

Anticipated Results

The students will understand how to arrive at and evaluate alternative solutions. They have successfully arrived at the pros and cons of each solution for their problem.

Illustration of Steps 2 and 3
of the Critical Thinking Process

The following illustration is a continuation of the discipline problem identified by a student support team in activity 1:

- Students have recorded their problem on step 1 of the Problem Solving Handout: Students feel hurt and angry when classmates verbally abuse them in the classroom and on school grounds.

- In step 2 the students brainstormed the following alternative solutions:

  use build-up statements to replace put-down statements

  say I-messages to confront a classmate rather than say negative "you" messages

  reprimand students by making them stay after school

  report students to the Dean

  design a behavioral contract for students not abiding by the Behavioral Code

- In step 3, students arrive at the pros and cons of each alternative solution.

Pros

1. Students motivate each other through positive statements.

2. Students don't feel threatened when confronted with I-messages.

3. Students don't like to stay after school. They will be conscious of not making negative comments.

4. Dean will give students after-school duties to perform on school grounds.

5. Student can change negative behavior to positive behavior via a behavioral contract.

Cons

1. Students have bad habits and can't think of positive things to say.

2. Students have difficulty putting together and saying I-messages.

3. Because of jobs and other activities, students will not stay after school.

4. Because of the large number of student referrals, students are delayed several days before seeing the Dean.

5. The teacher or counselor must take the time to meet with a student and complete a behavioral contract.

STEPS FOR IMPLEMENTING A DECISION HANDOUT

STEPS

1. Record your decision.

    • _____

    • _____

    • _____

2. List the steps to take to implement your decision.

    • _____

    • _____

    • _____

    • _____

3. List the barriers that could keep you from completing your steps.

    • _____

    • _____

    • _____

    • _____

4. List ways to overcome each of these barriers.

    • _____

    • _____

    • _____

    • _____

5. Set a deadline date for a follow-up meeting to check the progress made.

    Date: _____

6. Review the progress made and make recommendations for revisions or continue with the present plan. For more space, use the back of this form.

ACTIVITY 3

MAKING AND IMPLEMENTING A DECISION

STEPS 4, 5, AND 6 OF THE CRITICAL THINKING PROCESS

Purpose

To understand how to make and implement a decision to solve a particular problem.

Skill Development

The student will:

- ✓ learn how to make and implement a decision
- ✓ practice discussion and good communication techniques

Materials

- The *Six-Step Critical Thinking Process* handout (from activity 1)
- Paper pads and marking pens for recording items
- *Steps for Implementing a Decision* and *Six-Step Problem Solving Process* handouts (from activities 1 and 2)

Introduction (3 minutes)

The leader will introduce the activity as follows:

1. Explain to students that today they will review the pros and cons of each alternative solution from activity 2, decide on the best solutions, and design action plans to implement their teams' decisions.
2. Inform them that to complete this process they will complete steps 4 and 5 of the problem solving process.
3. Explain why steps 4 and 5 are important to the critical thinking process.
4. Refer the students to the critical-thinking chart handout.

Procedure (35 minutes)

The leader will conduct this activity as follows:

1. Ask each team to sit around a table, in circles on the floor, or turn their desks to face each other.

2. Ask students to bring their Problem Solving and Steps for Implementing a Decision handouts to their team meetings.

3. Ask the team facilitators to review and discuss the pros and cons of each alternative solution with their teams.

4. Tell students to share their personal experiences and the consequences that could result from the associated pro or con.

5. Based upon this discussion, ask each team to build a consensus as to which solution or solutions are the best.

6. Ask team members to record their teams' decisions on step 4 of the Problem-Solving handout.

7. Move on to step 5 and refer the students to the handout on Steps for Implementing a Decision. Ask them to record their decisions on step 1.

8. Ask the team facilitators to lead their teams through decision-making steps 2 through 5; remind the recorders to copy headings and answers on their paper pads, and tell the students to copy this information on their decision-making handouts.

9. Move from team to team and assist as needed.

Discussion (omit)

Appreciation (omit)

Instructional Tips

1. When students list the steps for implementing their decisions (step 2), they will need to know:
   - what they will need to do
   - how they will do it
   - when and where the activity will take place

2. Review of steps 3, 4, and 5 are self-explanatory.

3. For step 6 set a date for a progress review meeting.

4. Explain to the students that at this meeting they will check the progress made in the implementation of their action plans. They will also determine if revisions need to be made or to continue with the same plan.

Anticipated Results

Students will understand how to make and implement a decision for solving a problem. Students have successfully designed action plans for solving their problems. Students with behavioral problems will implement their action plans as indicated in the illustration of steps 4, 5, and 6 of this activity.

Illustration of Steps 4, 5, and 6 of the Critical Thinking Process

The following illustration is a continuation of the discipline problem identified in activity 1. In activity 2, a student support team arrived at alternative solutions for its problem and listed the pros and cons of each solution.

- In activity 3, the students decided on the best solution (step 4) to design a behavioral contract for students not abiding by the Behavioral Code.

- Team members record this decision on step 1 of the *Steps for Implementing a Decision* handout.

- Team members complete step 2, "List the Steps to Take to Implement Your Decision."

  —Each student will meet with the counselor to design a behavioral contract.

  —Each student will arrive at positive behavior to replace misbehavior.

  —Each student will agree to positive actions for executing positive behavior.

  —Each student and the counselor will set the consequences for future misbehavior.

  —Each student and the counselor will sign the contract and set a date for the progress review meeting.

- Team members complete step 3, "List the Barriers that Could Keep You from Completing Your Steps."

  —Negative pressure from peers to use put-down statements.

  —A bad habit of using negative language to abuse others verbally.

  —A lack of respect for others.

- Team members complete step 4, "List Ways to Overcome Each of These Barriers."

  —Become a team leader and practice positive peer pressure to motivate teammates.

  —Work on using build-up and I-message statements to replace put-down messages.

  —Show respect for others by abiding by the Behavioral Code.

- Team members complete step 5, "Set a Deadline Date for a Follow-Up Meeting to Check the Progress Made."

(continued on next page)

Illustration of Steps 4, 5, and 6
of the Critical Thinking Process
(continued)

Note that the deadline date and the progressive review meeting is the same as agreed to by each student and counselor for the Behavioral Contract.

- Team members complete step 6. Each student will meet with the counselor to review his/her progress and to receive recommendations from the counselor for revisions if needed.

Students are given two weeks (per the deadline date) to practice positive behavior in the classroom and on school grounds. The teacher, counselor, and student support team members will monitor each student's behavior. Students that are unable to meet the expected behavioral standards will have to endure the consequences specified in the behavioral contract. Through positive support and peer pressure from support team members, the student should meet the behavioral standards. Refer to the consequences for misbehavior in Section I.

Through this activity, students get the opportunity to implement an action plan.

ACTIVITY 4

HELPING A TEAMMATE SOLVE
A PERSONAL PROBLEM

Purpose

For each team to help a member solve a personal problem.

Skill Development

The student will learn how to:

✓ help a teammate solve a problem through team problem solving

✓ improve his/her problem solving skills

✓ enhance positive communication skills

Materials

- *Steps for Implementing a Decision* and *Six-Step Problem Solving* handouts (from reproducible copies within activities 1 and 2)
- Paper pads and marking pens for recording items

Introduction (2 minutes)

The leader will introduce this activity as follows:

1. Explain that today each team will use the problem solving process to help a teammate solve or cope better with a personal problem.
2. Remind them that they will help a teammate deal better with situations at school, home, or in the community.

Procedure (40 minutes)

1. Ask teams to sit around a table.
2. Ask for a volunteer from each team to lead this activity.
3. Instruct teams to review their list of problem areas from activity 1.
4. Remind teams of the importance of observing the confidentiality ground rule.
5. Locate a volunteer from each team who is experiencing one of these problems and wants help to solve his/her problem.
6. Ask the volunteers to discuss the specifics of his/her problem with their teammates.
7. Instruct the team leaders to refer to the problem-solving steps to guide their teams through this process, and to help their teammates solve their problems.
8. Ask the team recorders to record the six steps on their paper pads and record student input under the appropriate headings.
9. Pass out problem solving and decision making handouts to the affected students and instruct them to record pertinent data from the paper pads on their handouts during and after this activity.
10. Move from team to team and help as needed.
11. Follow through to be sure that students have copied the important steps for guidance and to help them cope with their problems. See the example at the end of this activity.
12. Remind the affected students that they are expected to implement their action plan. They will meet with their teams per the deadline date of step 5 to check the progress made.

Discussion (omit)

Appreciation (omit)

Instructional Tips

Discussions of a student's problems may become personal. Therefore, remind the students to carefully observe all the ground rules and to practice positive communication skills.

Note: If the students have successfully covered Sections I and II (bonding and good communication skills), they will be prepared to do a good job in helping a teammate solve his/her problem. In short, this activity should be very rewarding and worthwhile.

Anticipated Results

The students understand how to function as a team to help a teammate solve a personal problem. The students have helped a teammate formulate a plan for solving his/her problem.

Example of How to Help a Student Cope With a Problem

Problem: John is tardy or truant to school on a regular basis.
   Solutions:

1. Go to bed at a decent hour.
2. Use an alarm clock to wake in the morning.
3. Quit full-time job and get a part-time job in the afternoons.
4. Have parents rescind privileges at home for infractions.
5. Suspend John from school.

PROS AND CONS OF SOLUTION #3:

Pros

By quitting full-time job during night hours, John can get to bed earlier.

Cons

John will lose money that he needs to pay for his car.

(continued on next page)

Best solution: Quit full-time job and get part-time job in the afternoon. John can still make car payments with a part-time job.

Steps for Implementing Decision:

- Give employer two weeks notice.
- Find a part-time job and begin working within two weeks.
- Get to bed early and set an alarm clock.
- Get dressed, eat breakfast, and leave home by 7 A.M.

Barriers:

- John tends to procrastinate and might put off looking for a part-time job.
- John has a bad habit of watching T.V. and getting to bed late.
- John is an evening person and has trouble waking up in the morning.

Overcoming Barriers:

- Set a deadline for getting a part-time job within two weeks.
- Complete homework assignments and get to bed early.
- Ask family member to check when alarm clock goes off to be sure John gets out of bed.

Deadline for Follow-Up Meeting
Date: October 10, 1994
Result: John has successfully met his goal of getting to school on time on a regular basis.

ACTIVITY 5

SOLVING YOUR OWN PERSONAL PROBLEM

Purpose

To focus on how to solve your own problem.

Skill Development

The student will practice using the problem solving process to solve a personal problem.

Materials

- *Steps for Implementing a Decision* and *Six-Step Problem Solving* handouts (from reproducible copies within activities 1 and 2)

Introduction (2 minutes)

The leader will introduce this activity as follows:

1. Tell the students that today they will use the problem solving process to solve a problem of their own.
2. Explain that at times they will want or need help from others to solve a problem; other times, they will prefer to solve their own problem.

Procedure (30 minutes)

The leader will conduct this activity as follows:

1. Give all students the problem solving and decision making handouts.
2. Explain that students are generally faced with problems regarding school, peers, family, drugs, or economics. These are all examples of problem situations they can work on.
3. Ask the students to select a problem that is bothering them, and work individually at their desks to complete the steps outlined on the problem-solving and decision making forms.
4. Move around the room and assist students as necessary.

Discussion (10 minutes)

Ask for a volunteer from each team to lead a discussion by asking the following questions.

1. What problems did you have working by yourself?
2. How did you feel about arriving at your own plan for solving your problem?
3. Why is it important for you to arrive at your own problem-solving plan?
4. How did the previous problem solving activities help you get through today's activity?

Appreciation (omit)

Instructional Tips (omit)

Anticipated Results

Each student has successfully completed a plan for solving a personal problem.

ACTIVITY 6

HELPING OTHERS INDIVIDUALLY
AS A PEER COACH

Purpose

To understand the techniques that are necessary to help a teammate solve a personal problem.

Skill Development

The student will learn how to:

- ✓ help or coach a teammate solve a personal problem
- ✓ practice and improve the positive communication skills necessary to facilitate this process

Materials

- *Typical Problems That Teens Encounter* handout
- *Steps for Implementing a Decision* and *Six-Step Problem-Solving* handouts (from reproducible copies within activities 1 and 2)

Introduction (2 minutes)

The leader will introduce this activity as follows:

1. Explain to the students that today they will use the problem-solving process to help a teammate solve a personal problem.
2. Tell them by helping a teammate cope with a personal problem, he/she will be better equipped to deal with the rest of the situations in his/her life.
3. Explain that most students go to their peers for advice or someone to talk to. Today, they will practice good communication skills and the problem-solving process to help a teammate solve a personal problem.

Procedure (35 minutes)

The leader will conduct this activity as follows:

1. Ask students to meet in their teams.
2. Give the students the handout of *Typical Problems That Teens Encounter* found at the end of this activity.

3. Remind them that they can use these examples to get ideas for problems to pursue.

4. Ask students to pair off with a teammate and select a personal problem from the handout to work on.

5. Stress the fact that personal problems should be relevant to their present situation.

6. Ask one student to act as a peer helper and the other partner to practice the role of a student needing help.

7. Remind the peer helper to ask good open-ended questions and to use good listening skills as he/she goes through the six-step process.

8. Inform the student with the problem to record pertinent data on his/her problem-solving and decision-making forms.

9. Move around the room and assist as needed.

10. Ask each student to implement his/her action plan, and share the results of the plan with his/her peer helper on the deadline date of step 5.

11. Remind each student and his/her peer helper that during the progress review meeting they can revise each student's plan or stay on course.

Discussion (10 minutes)

Ask a volunteer from each team to lead a discussion by asking the following questions.

1. How did your peer helper help you cope with your problem?

2. What was the most difficult thing to do as a peer helper?

3. How did it feel to help a peer? Explain.

Instructional Tips

1. Tell peer helpers to share their experiences or the experiences of others as appropriate, to help the partner arrive at his/her solutions for coping with the problem.

Anticipated Results

The students have the confidence that they can help a teammate cope with a personal problem; they successfully help a teammate arrive at a plan for solving a personal problem.

EXAMPLES OF TYPICAL PROBLEMS
THAT TEENS ENCOUNTER

© 1995 by The Center for Applied Research in Education

SITUATION 1:

A friend of yours is ignoring you. What can you say or do to resume your friendship?

SITUATION 2:

Your parents forbid you to date a boy or girl friend that you like a lot. What can you say or do to let your parents know your friend is not a bad influence on you?

SITUATION 3:

You want to stop taking drugs with your friends. What can you say or do to let your friends know that you don't want to take drugs with them?

SITUATION 4:

Your teacher thinks you are lazy because you have a problem completing your daily school assignments. What can you do or say to let your teacher know that you need more individualized instruction or tutoring because you don't understand the assignments?

SITUATION 5:

A classmate constantly "puts you down" and gossips about you with others. What can you do or say to get this person to stop this negative behavior toward you?

ACTIVITY 7

USING THE CRITICAL THINKING PROCESS TO DEFINE AND CLARIFY A PERSONAL CONFLICT

Purpose

To understand the skills necessary to define and clarify a personal conflict.

Skill Development

The student will learn how to:

✓ define and clarify a personal conflict

✓ practice and improve brainstorming, discussion, and positive communication skills

Materials

- *Conflict Resolution Notes* handout
- *Conflict Resolution Guidelines* handout
- Paper pads and marking pens for recording brainstorming items and pens or pencils for recording notes.

Introduction (3 minutes)

The leader will introduce this activity as follows:

1. Tell the students that today they will learn how to define and clarify a personal conflict.
2. Explain that conflict is common among teenagers since they have different feelings and opinions about things.
3. Explain that when conflict evolves, they must learn to resolve conflict in a friendly and positive way.
4. Inform them that if they don't learn how to resolve conflict, they can hurt each other emotionally or physically.
5. Tell them a goal of this activity is to prevent them from hurting each other.

Procedure (45 minutes)

The leader will conduct this activity as follows:

1. Ask the students to meet in their teams.

2. Ask for volunteers from each team to act as a facilitator and a recorder.

3. Tell the facilitators to lead a brainstorming session to arrive at typical situations whereby peers get into conflict with each other.

4. Remind the recorders to copy these ideas on the paper pads.

5. At the conclusion of this activity ask the teams to select one conflict situation from their list; explain that they will use this conflict situation to role practice an activity with two students in conflict.

6. Ask for two student volunteers from the same team to work with you in a triad to illustrate how the conflict resolution process works.

7. Before beginning this demonstration, pass out handouts on *Conflict Resolution Guidelines* to all students.

8. Review step one: introduction and ground rules.

9. Illustrate the role of the mediator, and ask the students to role practice two students in conflict.

10. During this demonstration the mediator and students in conflict will refer to step 2 of their guidelines.

11. After this demonstration show the students how to record the definition of the conflict on the *Conflict Resolution Notes* handout. (Refer to step 2 of the guidelines.)

12. Next, ask for three volunteers from each team to role practice the conflict situation they selected from their brainstorming list.

13. Pass out *Conflict Resolution Notes* handout for recording their conflict definitions.

14. Remind them that the task of the mediator is to help the students in conflict to define and clarify their conflict, and to agree on a settlement.

15. Remind the mediator to ask open-ended questions to help the students define the conflict and express their feelings about the conflict.

16. Remind the students in conflict to use I-messages to express their feelings and refrain from using "you" messages.

17. Remind the mediators to use reflective listening skills to summarize the content and feelings of what both students said, and to continue this process until it is clear that both parties agree on the definition of their conflict.

18. Move from team to team and assist as needed.

19. Ask members from each triad to rotate and take turns as the mediator.

20. If time permits, ask for three more members from each team to role practice this activity, or continue this activity the following day until every student has practiced the role of the mediator.

Discussion

Ask a volunteer from each team to lead a discussion by asking the following questions:

1. What happened to cause the conflict?
2. How do you feel about what happened?
3. Explain why you feel the way you do.

Instructional Tips

1. During the role practicing demonstration ask the students to sit around a table with you. The table is used to print notes on.
2. To begin the demonstration, refer to step 2 of the guidelines and refer to the Discussion questions.
3. As the students answer the Discussion questions, print their answers on the Conflict Resolution Notes handout.
4. Ask the other team members to critique the demonstration, and describe the positive communication techniques that were effective in getting the students to define and clarify their conflict.
5. Monitor the teams carefully to determine when a triad has completed this activity, so you can get another triad to role practice this activity.

Anticipated Results

✓ The students understand how to define and clarify a personal conflict

✓ The students have effectively employed skills and techniques necessary to implement steps 1 and 2 of the critical-thinking process.

CONFLICT RESOLUTION GUIDELINES

STEPS

1. *Introduction and Ground Rules*

   Ask the students in conflict if they want to solve their problem. Have both parties agree to solve their problem before moving on to the next step.

   Explain and obtain agreement on each of the five ground rules:

   - Agree to solve the problem.

   - There is no arguing or use of "you" statements.

   - Students are to use I-statements.

   - Do not interrupt each other or the mediator.

   - Be honest and give direct answers to the questions.

2. *Define the Conflict*

   The mediator will question the most calm student first (person #1). Ask persons #1 and #2 the following questions:

   What happened to cause the conflict?

   How do you feel about what happened?

   Why do you feel this way?

   Record answers to these questions in the Conflict Resolution Notes. During the question and answer period use reflective listening and ask additional open-ended questions such as: *how long, how often, when, what do you mean,* and so on. Continue questioning until both parties agree upon the definition of the conflict. Record the definition.

3. *Finding a Solution*

   Ask persons #1 and #2 the following questions:

   What can *you* do to solve the conflict (not what you expect the other party to do)?

(continued on next page)

Ask a specific follow-up question that is directly related to each of the student's answers such as: *What can you do to stop the put-down messages?* Take notes and use reflective listening and ask additional questions, as needed.

4. *Deciding to Agree on the Best Solution*

   Ask persons #1 and #2 the following questions:

   What are the positive things about your solutions?

   What are the negative things about your solutions?

   Again, take notes and record the best solution.

5. *Agree to the Steps Necessary to Implement the Resolution*

   Ask both students to record their decision to resolve the conflict on step 1 of the Steps for Implementing a Decision handout. Move through steps 2 to 5 and ask the following questions:

   What steps will you need to take to resolve your conflict and implement your decision?

   What barriers could keep you from completing your steps?

   What are some ways to overcome these barriers?

   Take notes, use reflective listening, and ask additional questions as appropriate. Record the answers to the above questions on the Steps for Implementing a Decision handout. Set a date for a follow-up meeting.

6. Progress Review Follow-Up Meeting

   Conduct a progress review meeting to determine whether to continue with the original action plan or to make revisions. If revisions are necessary, revise and make changes on the steps of the original plan.

CONFLICT RESOLUTION NOTES

DEFINITION OF THE CONFLICT

Person #1: _____

_____

Person #2: _____

_____

Record the definition of the conflict: _____

_____

FINDING A SOLUTION TO THE CONFLICT
(list alternative solutions from persons #1 and #2)

Person #1: _____

_____

Person #2: _____

_____

AGREEING ON THE BEST SOLUTION

Persons #1 and #2 will discuss and weigh the positive and negative things about each alternative solution.

Person #1:

Positive: _____

_____

Negative: _____

_____

Person #2:

Positive: _____

_____

Negative: _____

_____

Record the best solution: _____

_____

ACTIVITY 8

FINDING AN AGREEABLE SOLUTION
TO A CONFLICT

Purpose

To understand the process necessary to resolve a conflict and agree on a solution.

Skill Development

The student will learn how to:

✓ resolve a conflict and agree to a solution

✓ practice and improve the positive communication skills needed to resolve a conflict

Materials

- *Conflict Resolution Guidelines* handout (from activity 7)
- *Conflict Resolution Notes* handout (from activity 7)
- *Conflict Resolution Agreement Form* handout

Introduction (1 minute)

The leader will introduce this activity as follows:

Explain that today students will learn how to reach an agreeable solution so that both parties will win.

Procedure (45 minutes)

The leader will conduct this activity as follows:

1. Ask the students to meet in their teams and bring their Conflict Resolution handouts with them.

2. Refer the students to steps 3 and 4 of their Conflict Resolution Guidelines handout and review these steps briefly.

3. Ask the same triad to meet with you to role practice steps 3 and 4, and refer to the Conflict Resolution Guidelines for directions.

4. Pick up from step 3 and role practice the same conflict situation.

5. After these students agree to a solution of their conflict, show them how to record this information on the Conflict Resolution Notes handout.

CONFLICT RESOLUTION AGREEMENT FORM

Date _____   Review Date _____

Name _____

Agrees: _____

_____

_____

_____

_____

_____

_____

_____

Name _____

Agrees: _____

_____

_____

_____

_____

_____

_____

_____

Signature _____   Date _____

Signature _____   Date _____

6. When this demonstration is over, ask the teams to form new triads and practice this same activity (via their situation selection) with each person taking turns as the mediator.

7. Move from team to team and assist as needed.

8. After teams have completed step 4, pass out copies of the Conflict Resolution Agreement Form to be completed next.

9. Instruct students to refer to step 4 to get the necessary information needed to print their agreement statements.

10. Tell students to record these statements on Agreement Forms stating what they agreed to do to resolve their conflict.

11. Ask the students to sign and date their forms.

Discussion (omit)

Appreciation (omit)

Instructional Tips

1. To begin the role-practicing demonstration, refer to step 3 (finding a solution) and ask both students this question: What can *you* do to solve the problem?

2. Record their answers on the Conflict Resolution Notes handout and then move on to step 4.

3. Review both answers with the students and ask them this question: What are the positive things about your solution?

4. Record their answers and then ask: What are the negative things about your solution?

5. Again, record their answers on the resolution notes.

6. After discussing and weighing the positive and negative aspects of their solutions, ask: What is the best solution?

7. Summarize their answers and arrive at a solution that is compatible to both parties.

8. Ask each party: "Do you agree with this solution?"

9. Continue this process until both students reach full agreement as to the best solution for solving their conflict.

10. Record their decision on step 4 of the Conflict Resolution Notes handout.

11. During this agreement process, use reflective listening and ask open-ended questions to get a good dialogue going between yourself and the students.

12. Each student and the teacher should keep a signed copy of the agreement form as a reminder of how both parties should interact in their relationships in or outside of school.

13. This agreement is a "mock" role practicing agreement.

Anticipated Results

✓ The students understand how to resolve a conflict and agree to a solution. The students have effectively executed steps 3 and 4 of this process to arrive at a resolution agreement.

ACTIVITY 9

IMPLEMENTING THE TERMS OF THE AGREEMENT

Purpose

To understand the process necessary to implement the terms of an agreement.

Skill Development

The student will learn how to:

✓ implement the terms of a resolution agreement

✓ practice and improve the positive communication skills needed to implement an agreement

Materials

- Paper pads and marking pens for recording items.
- *Steps for Resolving a Conflict* handout

Introduction (2 minutes)

The leader will introduce this activity as follows:

1. Tell the students that today they will learn how to implement the terms of their resolution agreement.

2. Explain to them that they will arrive at action plans and that these plans will give them the directions needed to successfully implement their resolution agreement.

Procedure (30 minutes)

The leader will introduce this activity as follows:

1. Ask the students to meet in their teams and sit around a table or cluster their desks.
2. Ask for volunteers from each team to act as facilitator and recorder.
3. Pass out copies of Steps for Resolving a Conflict handout.
4. Ask each recorder to record the heading of step 5 of the resolution guidelines: Steps for Resolving a Conflict. This heading is recorded on a paper pad.
5. Ask team members to refer to step 4 of their resolution notes and copy the best solution on step 1 of Steps for Resolving a Conflict handout.
6. Ask each team to brainstorm steps needed to implement their decision and have the recorder list these items under the heading.
7. Ask students to transfer items from this list to step 2 of Steps for Resolving a Conflict handout.
8. Ask the facilitators to continue with steps 3 to 5 by asking the following questions: What are the barriers that could keep you from completing your steps? What are some ways you can overcome these barriers?
9. Remind the students to copy the answers to these questions on their forms.
10. Remind the students that when implementing this resolution process, they will set a deadline date for a follow-up review meeting. At this meeting they will check their progress made via the action plan and make revisions or continue on the same course of action.
11. Tell the students that this follow-up review meeting will take place during a class period.

Discussion (10 minutes)

Ask each team facilitator to lead a team discussion by asking the following questions.

1. How can we use this conflict resolution process in class or on the school campus?
2. Who should be the mediator?
3. What are some positive things that could result from this resolution process?

STEPS FOR RESOLVING A CONFLICT

STEPS

1. Record your decision or resolution for solving the conflict:

   _____

   _____

   _____

2. List the steps to take to implement your decision or resolve your conflict:

   _____

   _____

   _____

   _____

   _____

3. List the barriers that could keep you from completing your steps:

   _____

   _____

   _____

   _____

   _____

4. List the ways to overcome each of these barriers:

   _____

   _____

   _____

   _____

   _____

5. Set a deadline date for a follow-up meeting to check progress made.

   Date: _____

6. Review progress made and make recommendations for revisions or continue with the present plan. For more space use the back of this form.

4. What can we do to get this conflict resolution process started in class or on the school campus?

5. How can we use conflict resolution to mediate a discipline problem between two students, or to resolve class discipline problems?

Appreciation (omit)

Instructional Tips

1. Remind the recorders to record the headings of steps 3 and 4 of the Steps for Resolving a Conflict handout and list the brainstorming items under these headings on the paper pad.

2. Remind students to copy these brainstorming items on steps 3 and 4 of their action plan forms.

3. Remind the students that they will use this process in class to resolve a conflict.

Anticipated Results

✓ The students will understand how to implement the terms of a resolution agreement since they have executed this process successfully.

✓ Through a collaborative effort, a student mediator prevented a discipline problem between two students from escalating into a violent situation.

ACTIVITY 10

CLARIFYING AND DEFINING MATERIAL FOR A RESEARCH REPORT

Purpose

To understand and practice the skills necessary to define and clarify material for a research report about tobacco, alcohol, and other drugs.

Skill Development

The student will learn how to:

✓ define and clarify material for a research report

✓ practice and improve facilitation and discussion techniques

Materials

- ✓ Discussion questions on a paper pad or blackboard
- ✓ 3 x 5 cards
- ✓ Pencils or pens

Introduction (5 minutes)

The leader will introduce this activity as follows:

1. Tell the students that they will form study teams to do a research report on drugs and alcohol. Explain that they will form these teams at a later date.
2. Explain that today they will define and clarify the definition of tobacco, alcohol, and other drugs. Stress to them that this is the first step in preparation for doing the report.
3. Remind the students that many of them have seen friends or relatives abuse themselves by taking tobacco, alcohol, and other drugs.
4. State that the purpose of this activity is to begin to make them better informed about the dangers of tobacco, alcohol, and other drugs in order to make intelligent decisions about their use (or rather, nonuse).

Procedure (35 minutes)

The leader will conduct this activity as follows:

1. Ask the students to meet in their teams.
2. Tell the students that today they will talk about what they know about tobacco, alcohol, and other drugs. They will also list questions about what they would like to learn about tobacco, alcohol, and other drugs.
3. Ask for a volunteer from each team to lead a discussion by asking the following questions:
   - How would you define the words drug and alcohol?
   - How do drugs and alcohol affect an individual?
   - Which drugs are legal or illegal?
   - Why do people use tobacco, drugs, or alcohol?
   - Are drugs or alcohol easy to get?
   - What are the dangers of tobacco, drugs, or alcohol?
4. After about twenty minutes of discussion, ask recorders from each team to put four headings on a paper pad or blackboard as follows: *tobacco, alcohol, marijuana, cocaine,* and *other drugs* (PCP, heroin, and so on).
5. Ask the students to call out questions that they have about any of these drugs and ask recorders from each team to list these questions under the proper headings.

6. If students run out of questions, add additional questions of your own to the list or ask open-ended questions to stimulate some ideas for further discussion.

7. Explain that sometimes we are reluctant to ask sensitive questions in front of others. Therefore, give students 3 x 5 cards to print questions on that are of a sensitive nature.

8. Move from team to team and assist as needed.

Discussion (omit)

Appreciation (omit)

Instructional Tips

1. In preparation for this activity, print the discussion questions on a paper pad or blackboard or type the discussion questions on a handout to give to each facilitator.

2. You can conduct this activity in teams or as a class. Use your discretion and select the method that will generate the most productive results.

3. Be prepared to answer questions or provide additional input about tobacco, alcohol, and other drugs during the discussion period.

Anticipated Results

Students will define and clarify what they know about tobacco, alcohol, and other drugs and what new facts they would like to learn about these substances.

ACTIVITY 11

GATHERING AND REVIEWING FACTS ABOUT TOBACCO, ALCOHOL, AND OTHER DRUGS

Note: It takes three class periods to cover activity 11. Therefore, the leader will introduce each day's activity and conduct the activity procedures as shown.

Purpose

To understand the process necessary to gather and review facts about tobacco, alcohol, and other drugs.

Skill Development

The student will learn how to:

✓ gather and review facts about tobacco, alcohol, and other drugs

✓ practice and improve the skills of working cooperatively in pairs and on study teams

✓ practice and improve the positive communication skills necessary to discuss, interpret, and share facts and information about these substances

Materials

- A list of questions to cover each topic
- Instructional materials to cover each topic, such as textbooks and other written materials covering tobacco, alcohol, and other drugs
- Paper and pencils or pens

CLASS PERIOD 1

Introduction (2 minutes)

The leader will introduce this activity as follows:

1. Tell the students that today they will begin working in pairs and study teams to gather information for answering questions about tobacco, alcohol, and other drugs.

2. Explain that by working in teams, they will have the help and support needed to gather and review facts and information for answering their questions and they will learn from each other.

Procedure (45 minutes)

The leader will conduct this activity as follows:

1. Ask the students to meet in their teams and pair off with a teammate.

2. Ask each pair to select a topic, such as alcohol, and give them the instructional materials needed to answer the questions on their topic.

3. Be sure that every topic is covered, including the aforementioned substances.

4. Pass out lists of questions covering each topic to the appropriate pair of students. (Refer to Instructional Tips)

5. Instruct each pair to divide their questions evenly and to answer the questions after reading the instructional materials.

6. Refer them to their list of questions and ask them to print the answers in the space under each question.

7. After each pair has answered all their questions, ask them to meet with other pairs working on the same topic to form study teams.

8. Ask for a volunteer from each team to act as a team facilitator.

9. Tell the facilitators to lead a discussion through the sharing of answers among teammates.

10. Inform students to ask additional questions for clarification. Continue this process until every student has a clear understanding of the answers to every question.

11. Remind students to copy any additional information needed along with the answers to the same questions.

12. Move from team to team and assist as needed.

Discussion (omit)

Appreciation (omit)

Instructional Tips

1. In preparation for this activity, review each team's category of drugs and compile one list of questions for each drug topic.

2. Type each list of questions on a handout and leave a space under each question for printing answers.

3. Get student volunteers to help you compile these lists of questions and to type the handouts.

4. Have the instructional materials ready to pass out to students.

5. Remind the study teams to discuss the answers to each question, one at a time, until each teammate has a clear understanding of the answers.

Another approach would be to assign study teams to conduct research on a drug topic of their choice. This method would simplify the organizational aspects of this activity. In addition, students with a keen interest in a drug topic are more apt to do a better job of researching the topic.

Either approach is sound and the teacher can select the method that is most appropriate for his/her classroom situation.

CLASS PERIOD 2

Note: In order to carry out this activity, the teacher must arrange for a guest speaker. It is recommended that the speaker be a physician with experience in the treatment and prevention of addiction to tobacco, alcohol, and other drugs.

Introduction (2 minutes)

The leader will introduce the activity as follows:

1. Explain to the students that an expert on drugs and alcohol will review each team's drug topic with them to:
   - confirm what they have learned
   - answer their questions
   - give them new information on their topics
2. Tell the students to bring their lists of questions in order to ask questions and record answers.

Procedure (50 minutes)

The leader will conduct this activity as follows:

1. Begin the activity by passing out blank copies of the original list of study questions to the appropriate study team members.
2. Remind the students to copy new information on these blank handouts under the appropriate questions.
3. Introduce the guest speaker to the students.
4. Ask each study team to sit together and ask questions of the speaker as a team.
5. Rotate the questions from team to team to keep all the students involved and interested in the activity.
6. Continue this process until every team has had a chance to have their questions answered.

Instructional Tips:

1. The teacher should talk to the speaker in advance of this activity and should agree on a presentation format.
2. The speaker could cover the latest or most up-to-date information on various drugs to stimulate interest.
3. A question and answer period should follow this presentation.

CLASS PERIOD 3

Introduction (2 minutes)

The leader will introduce this activity as follows:

1. Tell the students to meet with their study teams to review the new facts and information from the last class activity. Be sure that everyone has the right answers and understands the material.

2. Explain that they will share all answers and material with their permanent team members.

Procedure (45 minutes)

The leader will conduct this activity as follows:

1. Ask the students to meet in their study teams. Tell them to bring their lists of questions and answers to the meeting.

2. Ask for volunteers from each team to act as team facilitator.

3. Ask the facilitators to review and discuss any new answers to questions covering their topic with study team members.

4. During this oral review, remind teammates to ask additional questions. Ask facilitators to continue this review until all students have a clear understanding of the new material.

5. Remind the students to record this new information under the appropriate heading.

6. Rotate from team to team and assist as needed.

7. At the conclusion of this activity ask study team members to report to their permanent teams.

8. Ask for a volunteer from each team to act as a facilitator.

9. Ask the facilitators to lead a discussion with each pair—representing a different topic or sharing their topic with teammates.

10. Remind the team facilitators to allow time for questions and answers. This process will allow teammates to gain a clear understanding of each topic.

11. Continue this process until each team has covered every topic.

12. Move from team to team and help as necessary.

   Note: If necessary, take two class periods to cover this activity.

Instructional Tips

1. In preparation for this activity, get a complete set of questions and answers from each study team facilitator.

2. Make enough copies of these materials so that all students will have a set to cover each drug topic.

3. Pass out these materials to permanent team members before they begin their discussion of each drug topic.

Anticipated Results

✓ The students have gathered facts and information about specific drugs and alcohol. The students have reviewed and studied this information to gain an understanding of the subject.

ANALYSIS AND EVALUATION OF FACTS ABOUT TOBACCO, ALCOHOL, AND OTHER DRUGS

Purpose

To learn to analyze and evaluate information about tobacco, alcohol, and other drugs.

Skill Development

The student will learn how to:

✓ analyze and evaluate facts and information about these substances

✓ practice and improve facilitation, discussion, and positive communication techniques

Materials

- A list of questions and answers about tobacco, alcohol, and other drugs (Six-Step Problem Solving and Steps for Implementing a Decision handouts)
- Problem solving forms to record on (Reproducible copies from activities 1 and 2)
- Paper pads and marking pens to record items on

Introduction (2 minutes)

The leader will introduce this activity as follows:

1. Tell the students that today they will review their answers about tobacco, alcohol, and other drugs and arrive at alternative courses of action to take, such as abstaining from their use.

2. Explain to them that the facts and information they have studied will help them analyze and evaluate the effects of tobacco, alcohol, and other drugs on their bodies. This information will have a bearing on whether or not it is wise to take these substances.

Procedure (45 minutes)

1. Ask the students to meet in their teams.

2. Ask for volunteers from each team to act as facilitator and recorder.

3. Instruct the facilitators to lead a discussion about whether to take or not take tobacco, alcohol, and other drugs, and to arrive at negative and positive consequences resulting from these actions.

4. Ask the students to discuss this topic in general terms about whether to abstain or use tobacco, alcohol, and other drugs, and not to discuss this issue on a personal level regarding their own use or a teammate's of these substances.

5. Remind them that they will be giving their opinions about the use of these substances based upon their research report.

6. To facilitate this process, ask facilitators to discuss the following courses of action with their teams:

   • To use tobacco, alcohol, and other drugs

   • To abstain from using tobacco, alcohol, and other drugs

7. Ask the recorders to print the words (*Positive Consequences* and *Negative Consequences*) to the right of each of the topics, and to record these consequences accordingly as each team arrives at its information.

8. Direct the teams to refer to their list of questions and answers covering tobacco, alcohol, and other drugs. This approach will provide a basis for arriving at the consequences for taking the drugs.

9. Remind the teams to continue this discussion until they have arrived at all the possible consequences relating to taking or not taking these drugs.

10. Ask the team members to copy the courses of action and the positive and negative consequences on their problem solving form. (Six-Step Problem Solving handout)

11. Move from team to team and help as needed.

Instructional Tips

1. In preparation for this activity, ask the students to bring their notes covering all drug topics to the team meeting.

2. If necessary, demonstrate to all teams how to refer to these notes to arrive at positive or negative consequences.

3. If time permits, ask each team facilitator to share his/her team's positive and negative consequences with the other teams.

Anticipated Results

✓ The students understand how to analyze and evaluate facts and information.

✓ The students have arrived at a set of negative and positive consequences regarding the use of tobacco, alcohol, and other drugs.

ACTIVITY 13

MAKING AND IMPLEMENTING A DECISION ABOUT TOBACCO, ALCOHOL, AND OTHER DRUGS

Purpose

To become knowledgeable in how to make and implement a decision about tobacco, alcohol, and other drugs.

Skill Development

The student will learn how to:

✓ make and implement a decision

✓ practice and improve facilitation, discussion, and positive communication skills necessary to conduct this activity

Materials

• *Steps for Implementing a Decision* handout (from activity 2)
• Pens or pencils

Introduction (2 minutes)

The leader will introduce this activity as follows:

1. Tell the students that today they will decide on the best course of action to take regarding the use of tobacco, alcohol, and other drugs.

2. Explain that students will team up with other students making the same decision. Each team will complete an action plan for implementing its decision.

Procedure (45 minutes)

The leader will conduct this activity as follows:

1. Read each of the two courses of action to take and ask the students to vote on which course of action they believe is best.

2. Again, remind the students that their decisions are based on their opinions or beliefs about what is best for teenagers in general. They should not get on a personal level about what is best for them.

3. Pass out pieces of paper to the students and ask them to print their names and selected courses of action.

4. Collect the votes and call off the names of the students to form like study teams.

5. If all the students vote the same way, ask them to meet in their permanent teams.

6. After forming study teams pass out copies of the Steps for Implementing a Decision handout to every student. Ask them to print their decisions on step 1 of this form.

7. Ask for volunteers from each team to act as facilitator and recorder.

8. Instruct the recorders to copy the headings from the decision-making handout on the paper pads, and to record the brainstorming items under each heading.

9. Tell the facilitators to lead this brainstorming session to arrive at the steps needed to implement their courses of action.

10. Ask the students to copy these steps on their handouts.

11. Inform the facilitators to lead their teams through steps 2 to 5 to arrive at a plan of action.

12. Ask students to record brainstorming items of steps 2 to 5 on their handouts.

13. Rotate from team to team and assist as needed.

14. Remind them that on step 6 they will set a deadline for a progress review meeting. At that time they will decide to stay on the same course of action or make revisions accordingly.

Discussion (omit)

Appreciation (omit)

Instructional Tips

Because of peer pressure and the likelihood that some students will lie about abstaining from alcohol or drug use, the action plan is a "mock" plan. However, by experiencing this exercise, students will understand the steps they can take in the prevention of tobacco, alcohol, and other drug use.

Anticipated Results

✓ Students understand how to make and implement a decision.

✓ Students have completed an action plan that provides them with the directions to take for implementing their decisions.

ACTIVITY 14

SHARING AN ACTION PLAN WITH TEAM MEMBERS

Purpose

To share action plans with teammates to gain an understanding of their beliefs and feelings regarding the use of drugs and alcohol.

Skill Development

The students will learn how to:

✓ share an action plan with others

✓ practice and improve facilitation, discussion, and positive communication skills needed to conduct this activity.

Materials

- *Steps for Implementing a Decision* handouts that outline action plans
- A list of discussion questions printed on paper pads or handouts

Introduction (2 minutes)

The leader will introduce the activity as follows:

1. Inform the students that today they will share their action plans with their permanent teammates.

2. Explain that each student will explain their feelings and beliefs about why his/her plan is best for teenagers in general.

Procedure (35 minutes)

The leader will conduct this activity as follows:

1. Ask the students to meet in their permanent teams and to bring their action plans.

2. Ask students with the same action plan to sit together and share their plan with team members.

3. Remind the teams to follow the ground rules by respecting the beliefs of others and not criticizing others for having different opinions.

4. During this sharing period, tell the students to express new ideas to assist their teammates in the formation of their plans.

5. If every teammate arrives at the same plan of action, facilitators will lead a team discussion by asking the following questions:

   - How was it helpful to work with a study team?

   - Why will it become difficult to overcome the barriers in your plan?

   - Did the negative consequences of taking drugs have a bearing on your decision? Explain.

   - Do you believe that teenagers will be able to successfully execute your action plan? Explain.

Discussion (omit)

Appreciation (omit)

Instructional Tips

1. Move from team to team and provide positive reinforcement to your students. Compliment them for arriving at good plans for implementing their decisions.

2. Add additional input, as needed, to assist the students in their discussion process.

3. Pay particular attention to students with known drug problems to see how they relate to this activity, and observe their reactions.

4. Even though this is a "mock" activity, it is possible that a student "drug user" would be interested in executing his/her action plan. Accordingly, the teacher or counselor should talk to this student in private about implementing her/his action plan.

5. The counselor or teacher should use the six-step critical thinking process to change the behavior of students with discipline problems due to drug use. See the following illustration.

Anticipate Results

Through sharing action plans with each other, students have a good understanding of the feelings and beliefs behind each teammate's decision about whether teenagers should use or abstain from using alcohol or other drugs.

Note: Completing Sections I and II is a prerequisite for at-risk students in preparation for completing a cooperative research report. Bonding and communication activities provide at-risk students with the cooperative, interpersonal, and communication skills needed to complete this activity.

Example of a Student Deciding to Abstain from Using Alcohol and Other Drugs

After completing steps 1 to 4 of the Six-Step Problem-Solving Process handout, the student decides that the best solution is to abstain from using alcohol and other drugs. The student records this decision on step 1 of Steps For Implementing a Decision handout, as follows:

DECISION:

- To abstain from alcohol and drug use.

STEPS TO TAKE TO IMPLEMENT YOUR DECISION:

- Refuse to take drugs with peers.
- Get involved in playing football with new friends after school.
- Stay home at night and focus on completing homework assignments.
- Spend time on the weekend with family and new friends doing fun activities.
- Get counseling from an expert in alcohol and drug abuse.

(continued on next page)

BARRIERS:

- Peer pressure to take drugs.
- A lack of interest in other activities.
- Doesn't get along well with family members.
- Procrastinates about getting drug counseling.

WAYS TO OVERCOME BARRIERS:

- Get positive peer pressure to abstain from drug use from student support team.
- Review the results of the career/leisure assessment and select a job or activity to get involved in.
- Get and keep an appointment with a drug abuse counselor.

DEADLINE DATE: October 20, 1994

PROGRESS REVIEW MEETING:

Meet with the school counselor to check progress, make revisions, and stay on course.

ACTIVITY 15

DEFINE AND CLARIFY A DRUG PREVENTION PROJECT

Purpose

To define and clarify a drug prevention project.

Skill Development

The student will learn how to:

✓ define and clarify a drug prevention project

✓ improve and practice brainstorming, discussion, and communication skills necessary to conduct this activity

Materials

- Paper pads
- Marking pens

Introduction (2 minutes)

The leader will introduce this activity as follows:

1. Explain that there are discipline problems in school because of drug-related activities. The purpose of this project is to deter drug use and associated discipline problems from occurring at school.

2. Remind the students to consider how drug use relates to discipline problems as they brainstorm ideas for their drug prevention project.

3. Tell the students that today they will brainstorm some ideas for a drug prevention project.

4. Explain to them that their knowledge of the dangers of drugs and alcohol use provides the rationale for a project that combats drug abuse and discipline problems.

5. Explain that they will discuss various topics dealing with alcohol and other drugs to arrive at some ideas for the project.

Procedure (45 minutes)

The leader will conduct this activity as follows:

1. Ask students to meet in their teams.

2. Ask volunteers from each team to act as facilitator and recorder.

3. Tell the facilitators to lead a brainstorming session by asking the following questions.

   - Is there a drug problem in this school or in the community?
   - How do students get drugs?
   - Where do they go to get drugs?
   - How can a person abuse their health by taking drugs?
   - Do students in their school understand the dangers of taking alcohol and drugs?
   - How can we inform others about the danger of taking alcohol and drugs?
   - What has helped you the most to stay away from alcohol and drugs?
   - What kind of activities would you recommend to others for staying away from alcohol and drugs?

- How are drug-related activities connected to school discipline problems?
- How can we deter drug use and associated discipline problems simultaneously?

4. Ask the recorders to copy each question as a heading on their paper pads and to copy the brainstorming ideas under each heading.

5. Remind the facilitators to take one question at a time and get their team's input on one question before going on to the next question.

6. Move from team to team and assist as needed.

Discussion (omit)

Appreciation (omit)

Instructional Tips

1. In preparation for this activity, ask the students to review their notes and action plans relative to their research report on drugs and alcohol. This background information will prepare them for answering the questions in this activity.

2. Allow the students to provide the bulk of information in answering the questions. However, add information that is relevant to the topics.

3. Remember that you are a member of the class, as a team, and it is important for you to provide input to assist students in arriving at the best possible product.

4. In answering questions two and three, remind students that they do not have to provide specific names of people or places. Information indicating how or where students get drugs is sufficient.

Anticipated Results

The students will clarify the problem and brainstorm alternative solutions.

CONTINUATION OF ACTIVITY 15

Introduction (1 minute)

The leader will introduce this activity as follows:

1. Remind the students that they have brainstormed some good ideas for a drug prevention project.

2. Tell them that today they will decide on a top choice for their project which they will implement.

3. Remind them that their project should include measures to deter drug use and associated discipline problems.

Procedure (45 minutes)

The leader will conduct this activity as follows:

1. Ask the students to meet in their teams, and tell the facilitators and recorders to function in their same roles.
2. Direct each team to review the ideas under the last five questions and select the top three ideas for a drug prevention project. Ask for a hand vote or vote by secret ballot.
3. Tell the recorders to copy these ideas on a paper pad and record the words *pro* and *con* after each idea.
4. Next, ask each team to arrive at the pros and cons of each idea and to arrive at a top choice.
5. Remind the recorders to record this information under each pro and con heading.
6. Obtain the top choice from each team and put these choices on a paper pad or blackboard. If every team arrives at the same choice, it will not be necessary to go through a selection process.
7. Lead a class discussion or review these ideas and combine or eliminate ideas that are repetitive.
8. Ask the students, as a class, to discuss the pros and cons of each idea. Remind a recorder to record these ideas.
9. After this discussion, pass out pieces of paper and ask each student to print their top choice.
10. Count the number of votes for each idea and arrive at a top choice.

Discussion (omit)

Appreciation (omit)

Instructional Tips

If the discussion for a top choice slacks off, you can add information to provide insight to the pro and con issues.

Anticipated Results

The students have selected a drug prevention project which they will implement.

ACTIVITY 16

ARRIVING AT A GOAL STATEMENT
FOR THE DRUG PREVENTION PROJECT

Purpose

To understand the process necessary to arrive at a drug prevention goal.

Skill Development

The student will learn how to:

✓ set a drug prevention goal

✓ practice and improve discussion, brainstorming, and good communication skills needed to conduct this activity

Materials:

- Paper pads
- Marking pens

Introduction (1 minute)

The leader will introduce this activity as follows:

1. Tell the students that today they will decide on a goal as an end product for their drug prevention project.
2. Explain that this process will tell them what they hope to accomplish by completing their project.
3. Remind them that their goal statement should be directed at deterring discipline problems due to drug-related activities.

Procedure

The leader will conduct this activity as follows:

1. Ask the students to meet in their teams.
2. Have volunteers from each team act as facilitator and recorder.
3. Ask the team facilitators to lead a discussion by asking this question: "What do you hope to accomplish through this project?"

4. Ask the recorders to copy this question on a paper pad and then record their teammates' brainstorming ideas under this heading.

5. After each team has arrived at some ideas, facilitators will lead their teammates in summarizing and condensing their ideas into a succinct goal statement.

6. Assist each team in this process as explained in the instructional tips.

7. Move from team to team and help as necessary.

Instructional Tips

1. After each team has completed their list of brainstorming ideas, refer to one team's ideas and show the class how to recognize the main idea from each statement.

2. Ask the recorder to either underline or circle this main idea. Show the class how to combine or eliminate similar ideas to arrive at one statement.

   For example, in the following illustration "How can we inform others about the dangers of taking alcohol or other drugs," students could brainstorm the following ideas:

   - From *guest speakers*
   - From *experts* in the field
   - Through *counseling*
   - By watching *videotapes*
   - By reading *textbooks, newspapers,* or *magazines*

   Statement: Inform others about the dangers of drugs through counseling, videotapes, textbooks, newspapers, and magazines.

3. After this illustration, ask each team to continue in this same process.

4. Assist teams in this process as needed.

5. After each team has recognized and circled all the main ideas, you must move from team to team to help them combine these main ideas into one goal statement.

6. After each team has arrived at one goal statement, you will then meet with the class to determine its goal statement.

7. To arrive at one goal statement, you will use the same selection process as described in activity 16.

Anticipated Results

Students have arrived at a goal statement that specifies they will strive to deter drug use and drug-related discipline problems at school.

Note: The Goal Statement is included as an addition to the six-step process. This statement provides direction to the students as it describes what the students should accomplish by completing their project.

ACTIVITY 17

SELECTING TASKS FOR THE DRUG
PREVENTION PROJECT

Purpose

To understand and practice the process necessary to select and prioritize tasks
for a drug prevention project.

Skill Development

The student will learn how to:

✓ select and prioritize tasks

✓ practice and improve the facilitation, discussion, and communication skills
needed to conduct this activity

Materials

- Paper pads
- Marking pens

Introduction (1 minute)

The leader will introduce this activity as follows:
  Explain that today students will decide what it takes to complete their project. They will also decide which tasks are needed to conduct their project.

Procedure (45 minutes)

Today the leader will conduct this activity as follows:

1. Ask the students to meet in their teams, and get volunteers to act as facili-
   tators and recorders.
2. Direct the facilitators to lead a discussion by asking the following questions.
   - What resources will we need, such as people, supplies, and so on?
   - What methods or procedures will we need to complete this project?
   - Who will help us complete this project, such as specific community mem-
     bers, the media, and so forth?

- Where will we complete this project (school, community, neighborhood)?
- When will we do this project?
- What tasks or jobs will students need to do to complete this project?

3. Ask the recorders to copy the questions on their paper pads and record their teammates' ideas under each question.

4. Ask facilitators to take one question at a time to get ideas before moving on to the next question.

5. Ask each team to review the ideas that they listed under questions one to five to determine which tasks will need to be done to complete the project.

6. Accordingly, per question six, brainstorm tasks and ask the recorders to record these tasks on paper pads.

7. After this activity, ask a volunteer from each team to form a committee to compile the team's lists of tasks into one list of tasks.

Discussion (omit)

Appreciation (omit)

Instructional Tips

1. Move from team to team, or work with the teams as a class to discuss the questions and arrive at ideas.

2. Add your own ideas to provide input and complement the students' ideas.

3. Explain that the methods or procedures question relates to formulating a project action plan; describe the action plan as a schedule of tasks to be done by specific individuals within a specific period of time.

4. As the teams arrive at tasks to be done, add additional tasks if necessary to be sure all responsibilities are covered.

5. Assist the class committee, as needed, in arriving at one list of tasks.

Anticipated Results

The students have arrived at a list of tasks that are necessary to complete their drug prevention project.

DESIGNING AN ACTION PLAN
FOR A DRUG PREVENTION PROJECT

Purpose

To understand the process and skills necessary to design an action plan for completing a drug prevention project.

Skill Development

The student will learn how to:

✓ design an action plan for a drug prevention project

✓ practice and improve the positive communication skills needed to conduct this activity

Materials

- A list of tasks needed to complete the project
- *Project Plan* handouts to record tasks on

Introduction (1 minute)

The leader will introduce this activity as follows:

Tell the students that today they will design an action plan to give them the direction needed to implement their drug prevention project.

Procedure (35 minutes)

The leader will conduct this activity as follows:

1. Ask the students to meet as a class to review the drug prevention project tasks.

2. Pass out Project Work Plan handouts to the students. Ask them to copy the tasks from the paper pad, from activity 17, to the "Tasks and Resources" column of their work plan handout and to print their project goal statement from activity 16, as designated, on the work plan handout.

3. Ask students to volunteer to do the tasks listed on their work plan.

PROJECT WORK PLAN

PROJECT GOAL: _____

PROJECT NAME: _____

NAME	TASKS AND RESOURCES	DAY–MONTH–YEAR

4. Remind them that they can work individually, in pairs, or small groups to execute specific tasks. Review the tasks that lend well towards working in pairs or small groups.

5. As you find volunteers for tasks, ask the students to print the names of these students in the "Name" column of the work plan just opposite the task.

6. Ask the students to decide which tasks are to be done first and then prioritize tasks accordingly.

7. Set a time limit for task completion. Ask the students to record the expected date of completion for each task in the "Day, Month, Year" column of their work plan handout.

Discussion (omit)

Appreciation (omit)

Instructional Tips

1. In preparation for this activity, compile each team's lists of tasks onto one representative list.

2. Find student volunteers to help you with this task.

3. Record this list of tasks on a paper pad; students will refer to this list as they copy the tasks on their work plan handouts.

4. Also review the list of resources needed to complete the project from activity 18, and compile one list of resources.

5. As the students volunteer for tasks, ask them to refer to the list of resources. They will include the resources needed to do their tasks in the "Task and Resource" column of their work plans.

6. Assist the students to be sure they understand which resources they will need to do their specific tasks.

Anticipated Results

The students have selected their tasks, and have completed an action plan that is necessary to execute these tasks.

ACTIVITY 19

IMPLEMENTING A DRUG PREVENTION PROGRAM

Purpose

To understand how to implement a project work plan by executing team and individual tasks.

Skill Development

The student will learn how to complete specific tasks as a member of a work team.

Materials

Materials will be specified according to the needs of each task.

Introduction (3 minutes)

The leader will introduce this activity as follows:

1. Tell the students that today they will begin their project.
2. Remind them to review their project work plan responsibilities and ask questions about anything they don't understand before beginning the project.
3. Tell the students to put forth their best effort and together, as a team, they can complete an outstanding project that will benefit a lot of people.

Procedure (45 minutes)

1. Ask the students to meet in their work groups or to begin individually to complete their assigned tasks.
2. Monitor and assist students as needed.
3. Schedule planned work sessions during class time or after school until the project is completed. Pay close attention to time lines so that tasks are completed by the expected completion dates.

Discussion (omit)

Appreciation (omit)

Instructional Tips (omit)

Anticipated Results

The students have successfully implemented a drug prevention project to quell drug use and associated discipline problems on their school campus. Examples of drug prevention projects include:

1. A schoolwide media campaign to arouse an awareness about the dangers of drug use and associated discipline problems

   A media campaign might include the following:

   - Signs on school grounds
   - Articles in the local newspaper
   - Programs on the local T.V. station
   - Guest speakers for special school assemblies
   - Distributing information on where to go for drug counseling, prevention, and treatment programs
   - Viewing videotapes or films about the dangers of drug abuse
   - Articles in school newsletter or newspaper

2. Training students to provide positive peer pressure to refrain from drug activities or discipline problems on school grounds

   These activities would include:

   - Training students to support others through peer support teams
   - Training students to act as conflict resolution mediators to resolve conflicts on campus
   - Training students to act as peer helpers to help fellow students cope with personal problems relating to drug use or drug-related activities

   Note: Through the guidance of the teacher or counselor, student leaders would train other students in these peer support functions as well.

3. Student leaders organizing a meeting of students to design an action plan for preventing drug use and associated discipline problems from occurring in school

   This activity would include:

   - Using the six-step critical thinking process to obtain input from students to design an action plan for preventing drug use and associated discipline problems from occurring on the school grounds
   - Organizing peer support teams to implement the action plan

   Note: Sections I, II, and III of this guide can act as a vehicle to prepare students for the implementation of the aforementioned projects.

CAREER / LEISURE ACTIVITIES

INTRODUCTION

Discipline problems can erupt in the classroom due to negative behavior that originates in the community such as:

- students being truant from school because of participation in sexual activity, using drugs, and gang-related activities
- students purchasing drugs and guns in the community, and bringing these items to school

Consequently, the following discipline problems can occur in the classroom:

- a student reports to class under the influence of drugs
- a student shoots another student with a gun
- two students from rival gangs get into a fight

Students that are consistently truant become a discipline problem because administrators have to determine how to discipline these students. Should these students be suspended from school, or how do teachers and counselors motivate these students to attend class on a regular basis?

When discipline problems occur in the classroom as indicated above, the teacher can intervene as described in *Step 4—Intervening to Discipline a Student* in Section 1. However, this guide recommends that the teacher and counselor look at the "big picture" and make an effort to change the negative behavior of at-risk youths in the community. This should be done as a measure to prevent students from bringing drugs, guns, and gang-related problems to school, and deter associated discipline problems from developing in the classroom.

Through the activities in Section IV, the teacher and/or counselor collaborate with the students to prevent classroom discipline problems that originate in the community. Accordingly, they arrive at a plan to replace counterproductive activities with positive and productive career/leisure activities. For example, most at-risk students are interested in getting a part-time job. Therefore, this is an incentive to participate in the career assessment and exploration activities. Through taking the leisure interest survey, many at-risk students renew their interest in participating in football, basketball, baseball, and so forth. To participate in sports, students must attend school and maintain a C letter grade average or better. This leverage to stay in school to participate in sports has motivated many at-risk students to stay off the streets. Successful high school athletes can set such goals as obtaining an athletic scholarship to college and later playing professional athletics. These additional incentives can provide further motivation to succeed in school and in sports.

Through the effective implementation of Section IV, students are motivated to spend their time in productive career/leisure interest activities. They do not have the time or inclination to participate in counterproductive activities that can result in discipline problems in the classroom.

Sections II and IIII augment Section IV, since students have learned positive communication and critical thinking skills necessary to change their negative behavior in the community and prevent discipline problems from occurring in the classroom.

The following approaches are recommended for conducting Section IV.

1. The subject area teacher would identify students with discipline problems, as described in this introduction, and refer these students to a counselor. The counselor would pull Sections II, III, and IV from this guide to:

   - teach at-risk students how to prevent discipline problems from occurring in the classroom by learning and practicing positive communication and critical thinking skills

   - get at-risk students involved in positive career/leisure after school activities to replace sex, drug, and gang-related activities in the community.

2. Within a self-contained class that meets from four to five class periods each day, the teacher can use one class period each day over a semester time span to teach Sections I, II, III, and IV. It is recommended that a counselor assist the teacher with Section IV, since counselors have access to community agencies that provide jobs and leisure activities to youths. Depending on availability, the counselor can conduct this unit in the classroom or after school in a counseling group.

With both approaches, the counselor would coordinate with the teacher to keep abreast of the students' behavior in class, and support the teacher if discipline problems occur.

Through a team process each student collaborates with the teacher, counselor, and student support team members to prevent discipline problems in the classroom that originate from bringing guns, drugs, or gang-related problems into the classroom. This collaborative process improves the Collaborative Discipline Program.

This section should be used selectively by counselors who work with at-risk students who bring problems from the community that cause discipline problems in the classroom. An example would be an inner-city situation where gangs, drugs, and violence prevail. Accordingly, Section IV can be used effectively by a counselor to prevent discipline problems from happening in the classroom. This section is designed so that counselors can easily remove it and use it exclusively as a prevention program to deter discipline problems on the school grounds and in the classroom.

ACTIVITY 1

BRINGING DISCIPLINE PROBLEMS
FROM THE COMMUNITY TO SCHOOL

Purpose

To understand why bringing drugs, guns, and gang-related problems to school can cause discipline problems in the classroom.

Skill Development

The students will practice and improve communication and critical thinking skills through brainstorming, discussion, and decision making activities.

Materials

- A paper pad to record brainstorming items
- Marking pen

Introduction (5 minutes)

The leader will introduce this activity as follows:

1. Tell the students that today they will discuss how bringing drugs, guns, and gang-related problems to school can cause discipline problems.
2. Inform them that they will arrive at ways to change their negative behavior and activities by getting involved in productive and worthwhile career and leisure activities in the community.
3. Remind them that they will use positive communication and critical thinking skills to make good decisions about how to replace negative behavior with positive behavior.

Procedure (30 minutes)

The leader will conduct this activity as follows:

1. Lead a brainstorming session by asking the students to list discipline problems that can occur by bringing drugs, guns, and gang-related problems to school. Include how becoming pregnant or obtaining a disease from sexual intercourse can cause truancy-related discipline problems in school.

2. Ask a volunteer to record these brainstorming items on a paper pad and to leave room under each item/problem.

3. After completing the list of discipline problems, discuss the negative consequences that can result from each problem.

4. Tell the recorder to record the negative consequences under each problem.

5. Ask the students to discuss how these negative consequences will deter them from success in school.

6. Ask the students to list reasons why it is important for them to succeed in school. Be sure to stress the importance of graduating from high school to get a better paying job (than the typical high school drop-out).

7. Ask the students to list positive and productive activities that they could participate in after school to replace the negative activities involving drugs, guns, sex, and gang related activities in the community.

8. Tell the recorder to list these items.

9. Ask the students to discuss how participation in these activities could help them refrain from their other activities.

10. Remind them that a goal of Section IV is to get each student involved in a positive career or leisure interest activity after school.

Discussion (omit)

Appreciation (omit)

Instructional Tips

1. If this activity is covered in a self-contained classroom, the teacher or counselor and student support teams will facilitate this activity as previously described in Sections I, II, and III.

2. If students are referred to a counselor, the counselor can lead this activity or divide the students into teams. For 12 or more students, it is recommended that the students be divided into teams. Students who have participated in Sections II and III, a requirement for this activity, will be familiar with how to take the lead.

Anticipated Results

✓ The students understand why bringing drugs, guns, and gang-related problems to school can cause discipline problems. The students understand why replacing these negative activities with positive after-school career/leisure activities can prevent discipline problems in the classroom.

REINFORCING POSITIVE BEHAVIOR IN THE COMMUNITY

Purpose

To reinforce why it is important to replace drug use, violence via gun usage, and gang-related activities in the community with positive career/leisure activities.

Skill Development

The students will gain an understanding of why it is important to be productive citizens who are respected in their community.

Materials (omit)

Introduction (3 minutes)

The leader will introduce this activity as follows:

1. Explain to the students that today they will hear success stories from outstanding citizens in the community.
2. Inform the students that when these men and women were in high school they had similar discipline problems, but successfully overcame them to graduate from high school and get a good job. **Note:** If the speaker graduated from college, add this information to the introduction.
3. Remind the students to be polite and to give the guest speakers their full attention.

Procedure (45 minutes)

The leader will conduct this activity as follows:

1. Introduce each speaker and allow him/her to tell his/her story.
2. At the end of each talk, provide some time for the students to ask questions and carry on a brief dialog with the speaker.
3. Monitor this time limit to be sure each speaker has adequate time to tell his/her story and answer questions.

Discussion (omit)

Appreciation (omit)

Instructional Tips

1. Contact the following agencies, organizations, or people to locate guest speakers for this activity.

   - Community youth employment agencies that have contact with local employers

   - Local community service organizations, such as the Lions or Kiwanis Service Clubs, that are composed of local businessmen

   - Local university athletic department or local professional sports organization that provides outstanding athletes as guest speakers

   - Recent high school graduates who have good jobs and are respected citizens in the community

   - Social Service agencies that provide rehabilitation services to drug addicts and individuals on parole from prison, to locate individuals who have successfully overcome drug abuse or criminal problems to obtain pivotal positions in the community

2. Select individuals who have successfully overcome difficult problems in life to become respected citizens in the community. Try to locate known speakers who have a reputation for motivating young people to succeed in life.

3. To add variety to the program, select two or three speakers. Select speakers who are compatible with your students. For example, if the students represent a high percentage of an ethnic group, make an effort to locate speakers who represent these students. If you have female students in the class, locate successful women from the business community.

4. In advance of the program, make each speaker aware of the discipline problems the students have had in the classroom. Ask each speaker to relate to discipline problems he/she had in school and how he/she overcame them to graduate and succeed in life.

Anticipated Results

The students have gained a clear understanding from the guest speakers about the importance of overcoming discipline problems in the classroom in order to graduate from high school and get a good job.

ACTIVITY 3

TAKING WRITTEN AND CAREER SURVEYS

Purpose

To assess each student's career and leisure interests, abilities, and values.

Skill Development

The students will learn how to assess their career and leisure interests, values, and abilities.

Materials

- *COPS, CAPS and COPES Career Surveys*™ (See Instructional Tips)
- *Leisure Activity Surveys*
- Pencils or pens

Introduction (2 minutes)

The leader will introduce the activity as follows:

1. Explain that in the next four days students will complete career and leisure activity surveys.
2. Remind students that the purpose of this activity is for them to become aware of jobs and leisure activities they would like to participate in to replace negative behavior.
3. Stress the need for participation in positive career/leisure activities as a deterrent for discipline problems finding their way from community to classroom.
4. Inform the students that a goal of this unit is to get them involved in after-school jobs or leisure activities.

Procedure (Four class periods)

The leader will conduct this activity as follows:

1. Ask the students to meet in their teams.
2. Pass out the career and leisure activity surveys as follows:
   - On day one, pass out the COPS Career Interest Survey.
   - On day two, pass out the COPES Career Values Survey.
   - On day three, pass out the CAPS Career Ability Survey.
   - On day four, pass out the Leisure Activity Survey.

3. Refer the students to the directions on each survey. Explain and answer questions before students begin taking the surveys.

Discussion (20 minutes)

After the students have completed the career and leisure activity surveys, the leader will conduct a discussion by asking the following questions.

- Did anyone become aware of personal career or leisure interests, values, or abilities that were new to you?
- Why is it important to make the most of your special talents and abilities?
- Why is it tragic when individuals mess up their lives by taking drugs or harming others through violent activity?
- How can participation in career or leisure activities of your choice help you to make the most of your special talents and to refrain from drug abuse or violent activity?

Appreciation (omit)

Instructional Tips

1. When utilizing other career assessment surveys, students must have the latitude to select three career fields and three jobs within each field. This selection process takes place as described in activity 4.

2. *The Educational and Industrial Training Service* (EdITS) publishes the COPS, CAPS, and COPES Career Surveys™. EdITS provides a comprehensive assessment that matches a student's career interests, abilities, and work values with compatible career fields. To ease the administration of this assessment program the student will:
   - follow the directions given on the Comprehensive Career Guide form and from the survey forms
   - complete the surveys
   - score their own surveys

3. Refer to the resource index at the back of this guide for the address and phone number for EdITS. However, other career assessment surveys can be used to serve the same purpose. The Leisure Activity Survey contained in this guide is designed for this program specifically.

Anticipated Results

✓ The students have assessed their career and leisure interests, values, and abilities. The students understand why participation in career and leisure activities can divert them from drug- and gang-related activities.

LEISURE ACTIVITY SURVEY

NAME _____ DATE _____

Indicate your interest or lack of interest for each of the following activities by using this scale:

> 2: Record a 2 before an activity that is very interesting to you.
>
> 1: Record a 1 before an activity that might be interesting to you.
>
> 0: Record a 0 before an activity that is not interesting to you.

Review your scores and select the three leisure activity fields that interest you the most. Next, choose three activities from each of the three leisure fields.

INDIVIDUAL SPORTS

___ Auto Racing
___ Archery
___ Badminton
___ Bowling
___ Boxing
___ Canoeing
___ Cross-country
___ Fencing
___ Fishing
___ Golf
___ Gymnastics
___ Horseback Riding
___ Hunting
___ Ice Skating
___ Marksmanship
___ Motorcycling
___ Motorboating
___ Rowing/Boating
___ Sailing
___ Skin Diving
___ Snow skiing
___ Squash/Handball
___ Swimming
___ Surfboarding
___ Tennis
___ Water-skiing
___ Water-surfing
___ Wrestling
___ _____
___ _____
___ _____

TEAM SPORTS

___ Basketball
___ Baseball/Softball
___ Football
___ Ice Hockey
___ Rugby
___ Soccer
___ Track and Field
___ Volleyball
___ Water Polo
___ _____
___ _____
___ _____

PHYSICAL FITNESS

___ Aerobics
___ Backpacking
___ Bicycling
___ Exercising
___ Hiking/Walking
___ Jogging
___ Mountain Climbing
___ Rock Climbing
___ Roller Skating
___ Weight Training
___ Body Building
___ _____
___ _____
___ _____

GAMES

___ Billiards/Pool
___ Crossword Puzzles
___ Checkers
___ Chess
___ Computer Games
___ Horseshoes
___ Jigsaw Puzzles
___ Playing Cards/
     Bridge/Poker
___ Shuffle Board
___ Table Tennis
___ _____
___ _____
___ _____

CREATIVE ARTS

___ Arts and Crafts
___ Acting/Dramatics
___ Cooking/Baking
___ Ceramics/Pottery
___ Dancing/Social/
     Ballet/Square
___ Designing Clothing,
     Houses,
     Landscapes,
     Flower Arranging
___ Drawing/Painting
___ Interior Decorating
___ Jewelry Making
___ Leather Working

(continued on next page)

___ Photography
___ Playing Musical
    Instruments
___ Singing
___ Sculpture
___ Writing Stories,
    Poetry, Articles

___ _____
___ _____
___ _____

SOCIAL

___ Attending: Movies,
    Concerts, Plays,
    Lectures
___ Boy Scouts
___ Camping
___ Dining Out
___ Support Groups
___ Fraternal
    Organizations
___ Girl Scouts
___ Traveling
___ Visiting Friends
___ Visiting Museums
___ Dating

___ _____
___ _____
___ _____

MECHANICAL

___ Amateur Radio
___ Auto Repair
___ Cabinet Making
___ Computer
    Programming
___ Carpentry
___ Electronics
___ Metal Work
___ Repair/Maintaining
    Appliances

___ _____
___ _____
___ _____

HOBBIES

___ Bird Watching
___ Collecting Coins,
    Antiques
___ Gardening
___ Kite Flying
___ Knitting/Crocheting
___ Listening to Radio,
    Records/Tapes
___ Model Building
___ Needlework
___ Reading Books/
    Plays/Poetry

___ Sewing
___ Sightseeing
___ Sun Bathing
___ Watching T.V.
___ Watching Sporting
    Events
___ Weaving
___ Window Shopping
___ Caring for a Pet

___ _____
___ _____
___ _____

SERVICES

___ Civic Organizations
___ Conservation/
    Ecology
    Organizations
___ Political Activities
___ Religious Activities
___ Volunteer: Hospitals,
    Elderly, Schools,
    Social Agencies

___ _____
___ _____
___ _____

Review your scores and select the three leisure activity fields that interest you the most. Next, choose three activities from each of the three leisure fields.

ACTIVITY 4

SELECTION OF CAREER AND LEISURE FIELDS

Purpose

To select career and leisure activity fields that are compatible with each student's interests, values, and abilities.

Skill Development

The student will learn how to interpret and select jobs and leisure activities of his/her choice.

Materials

- The *COPS, CAPS, and COPES Career Surveys*™ and *Leisure Activity Surveys* for review of scores (see Instructional Tips)
- The *Comprehensive Career Guide for the COPS, CAPS,* and *COPES Career Survey*™ on which to record scores
- *Summary Check-Off Form*
- Pencils or pens

Introduction (2 minutes)

The leader will introduce this activity as follows:

1. Explain to the students that today they will review their scores from each survey. They will select three career and leisure activity fields.
2. Tell them they will pick the three most interesting jobs and leisure activities from each major field.
3. Remind the students that they will meet in teams, but they will complete this assignment individually. However, if necessary, team members can assist each other with this task.

Procedure (35 minutes)

The leader will conduct this activity as follows:

1. Ask the students to meet in their teams.
2. Instruct them in how to record their scores from the COPS, COPES, and CAPS surveys on page 2 of the *Comprehensive Career Guide.*

3. Explain how to interpret their top scores and then select their three best career fields (fields that are compatible with their interests, abilities, and work values).

4. Explain how to locate their career field selections on pages 5 to 11 of the Comprehensive Career Guide.

5. Ask the students to review a listing of jobs under each career field and pick three jobs from each field that are the most appealing.

6. Ask the students to review their leisure surveys and select the three most interesting leisure activity fields. Then they must select three activities from each field.

7. Pass out summary check-off forms to all students.

8. Instruct the students in how to record their career and leisure fields, jobs, and activities on the Summary Check-Off Form.

Discussion

The leader will conduct this discussion by asking the following questions:

- What is the most interesting thing that you learned about a career or leisure choice?

- How can you benefit from participation in a job or leisure activity selection?

- How can participation in a career or leisure activity divert you from bringing drugs or gang-related problems to school?

- How can this change in behavior prevent discipline problems from occurring in the classroom?

Appreciation (omit)

Instructional Tips

1. In advance, review the jobs listed under each career field on pages 5 to 11 of the *Comprehensive Career Guide,* and be prepared to define the job terminology and discuss what a worker does on various jobs. Refer to the *Occupational Outlook Handbook* or the *Dictionary of Occupational Titles* for job references.

2. When using other career assessment surveys, students will select their top three career fields and the three most interesting jobs from each field. They will then copy this information on the Summary Check-Off Form.

Anticipated Results

✓ The students are aware of their career and leisure activity values, interests, and abilities, and they have selected jobs and leisure activities that are compatible with their interests, values, and abilities. The students understand how participation in a job or leisure activity can divert them from bringing drug or gang-related problems into the classroom.

© 1995 by The Center for Applied Research in Education

SUMMARY CHECK OFF FORM

SATISFACTION

TEAMWORK	MONEY	INDIVIDUAL WORK	PRESTIGE	SERVICE	LEADERSHIP	COMPETITION	INDEPENDENCE	PHYSICAL EFFORT

ABILITIES

CRITICAL THINKING	CREATIVE	MECHANICAL	ATHLETIC	SOCIAL	LEADERSHIP	INTELLECTUAL

ENVIRONMENT

OUTDOOR	INDOOR	URBAN	RURAL	DESERT	MOUNTAINS	WATER	COASTAL

DATA	PEOPLE	THINGS

CAREER FIELDS
1.
2.
3.

LEISURE FIELDS
1.
2.
3.

ACTIVITY 5

UNDERSTANDING WHY STUDENTS RELATE TO JOBS AND LEISURE CHOICES

Purpose

To understand why students relate to and choose specific jobs and leisure activity choices.

Skill Development

The students will:

✓ understand why they prefer specific jobs or leisure activities
✓ practice using open-ended questions and reflective listening techniques

Materials

- Summary Check-Off Forms from activity 4
- Personal Selections Form
- Pencils or pens

Introduction (3 minutes)

The leader will introduce this activity as follows:

1. Explain to the students that today they will share their jobs and leisure activity selections with their teammates. They will become aware of each other's interests and connect to others with similar interests.
2. Inform them that they will also become aware of why they like certain jobs or leisure activities. For example, if they have mechanical ability they would enjoy auto repair, or if they have athletic ability they would enjoy playing sports.
3. Remind the students that as they become aware of job or leisure activity choices, they will be better equipped to select a job or leisure activity to replace negative activities.

Procedure (45 minutes)

The leader will conduct this activity as follows:

1. Ask the students to meet in their teams.

2. Ask for a volunteer from each team to lead a discussion by asking the following questions:

   - Why does your job or leisure choice appeal to you?

   - Have you ever participated in your job or leisure selections? Describe what it was like.

   - Can you tell us anything special about your job or leisure choices?

   - What new things would you like to learn about your career or leisure choices?

3. If students hesitate to share, you can begin by sharing your own job and leisure activity interests to stimulate conversation. Others with like interests will usually get involved in the discussion.

4. Remind students to ask open-ended questions and use reflective listening techniques.

5. After ten minutes of conversation, pass out copies of the *Personal Selections Form* to all students.

6. Refer to the *Data–People–Things* categories and explain as follows:

   - *Data* means working with ideas, information, words, or numbers (like a writer, accountant, or computer programmer).

   - *People* refers to jobs or leisure activities that involve direct contact with people (counselor, teacher, or nurse).

   - *Things* means the handling or manipulating of tools or machinery (carpenter or mechanic).

7. Instruct the students to look at the definitions of Data–People–Things and select a category or categories that are the most appealing for work and leisure.

8. Explain that students with multiple interests can select combinations, such as *Data/People* for a job or *People/Things* for leisure. They can also pick one category, such as *People* for work and *Things* for leisure.

9. Ask the students to print their selections over the job and leisure headings on the form.

10. Move on to the *Environment* category. Explain that each student will feel the most comfortable in a specific environment, and it is great if they can work and play in this environment.

11. Ask students to review the environmental setting choices and select the environment they would prefer for work and leisure.

12. Tell them to record their choices over the job and leisure headings for this category. Remind them that they can choose multiple combinations such as coastal/mountains for leisure.

13. Refer the students to the *Abilities* section.

14. Explain that each student is a unique person with special abilities—an awareness of these abilities will help he/she choose the appropriate job and leisure selections.

15. Follow the same procedures for selecting and recording information over the proper headings.

16. Refer to the *Satisfaction* category.

17. Explain that many people don't like their jobs and some people get bored during their leisure hours. Remind them that to live a happy and productive life it is important to get satisfaction from work and play.

18. Again, have the students follow the same selection and recording procedures for this category.

19. Complete this activity by having team members share their various category selections with their teammates. If necessary, take an additional class period for sharing this information. Refer to the *Discussion* section.

Discussion (10 minutes)

Ask for a volunteer from each team to lead a discussion by asking the following questions:

- Why are you a *Data, People,* or *Things* person?
- Why do you prefer a certain *Environment* for work or play?
- Describe why your *Abilities* lend well to a specific job.
- Why does a specific *Satisfaction* appeal to you the most?

Appreciation (omit)

Instructional Tips

1. Be prepared to explain each category and answer questions.

2. Give examples of combination selections, such as a carpenter that enjoys building a home with a team of workers, which is a People/Things combination.

3. Encourage students to share their selections with teammates. Remind them to ask good open-ended questions and to use reflective listening techniques.

Anticipated Results

✓ The students understand why they prefer specific jobs and leisure activities. The students have selected job and leisure activity satisfaction categories that clearly define their job and leisure preferences.

PERSONAL SELECTIONS FORM

DATA–PEOPLE–THINGS

Choose the category that best matches your job and leisure interests.

Definition: Data–People–Things
Data: Refers to gaining information and ideas by seeing, searching, interpreting, and includes working with numbers, words, symbols, ideas, and concepts.
People: Refers to assisting, instructing, counseling, guiding, supervising, directing, and leading people.
Things: Refers to manipulating and handling objects or things like machines, tools, and equipment.

_____   _____
Job   Leisure

ENVIRONMENT

Choose the most appealing category for a job or leisure environment such as: Outdoor, Indoor, Urban, Rural, Desert, Mountains, Water, and Coastal.

Definition: Environment
Outdoor: Outside a building.
Indoor: Inside a building.
Urban: A city dwelling with many buildings and people.
Rural: A country setting with few people or buildings.
Desert: A hot and dry climate with sandy terrain.
Mountains: High altitude and terrain with trees and snow.
Coastal: Beach or water front near an ocean, lake, or river.
Water: On top of or underneath an ocean, lake, river, or swimming pool.

_____   _____
Job   Leisure

ABILITIES

Choose your abilities that match best with a job and a leisure activity such as: Critical Thinking, Creative, Mechanical, Athletic, Social, Intellectual, and Leadership.

Definition: Abilities
Leadership: Leading and motivating others to high achievement.
Critical Thinking: Organizing, compiling, and analyzing ideas, information, and data.
Creative: Originating creative works of art, music, writing, drama, and invention.
Mechanical: Manipulating and handling machinery and tools.
Athletic: Performing well in athletic sports.
Social: Relates well with other people.
Intellectual: A high level of reasoning and logical thinking.
Communication: Listens and verbalizes well with others.

_____   _____
Job   Leisure

SATISFACTION

Choose the most appealing satisfaction that could be obtained from a job and a leisure activity such as: Teamwork, Money, Individual work, Prestige, Service, Leadership, Independence, Physical Effort, Competition.

Definition: Satisfaction
Teamwork: Working with members of a team.
Money: Earning dollars and cents.
Individual Work: Working on an individual task or job.
Prestige: Recognized as being an important person.
Service: Providing service to others.
Leadership: Directing, guiding, and persuading others.
Independence: Working independently and making own decisions.
Physical Effort: Physical exertion to perform a task.
Competition: Applying one's abilities against another.

_____   _____
Job   Leisure

ACTIVITY 6

UNDERSTANDING JOB
AND LEISURE ACTIVITY CHOICES

Purpose:

To understand how job satisfaction correlates with job and leisure activity choices.

Skill Development

The student will learn how to correlate job satisfaction with job and leisure activity choices.

Materials:

- *Personal Selection Form* (from activity 5)
- *Summary Check-Off Form* (from activity 4)
- Pens and pencils

Introduction (2 minutes)

The leader will introduce this activity as follows:

1. Explain that today they will gain an understanding of how job satisfaction correlates with job and leisure activity choices.
2. Illustrate by giving examples as follows:
   - a data person could be interested in being a writer
   - a people person could be interested in being a physician

Procedure (35 minutes)

The leader will conduct this activity as follows:

1. Ask the students to meet in their teams.
2. Instruct them in how to transfer information from their *Personal Selection Form* (PSF) to their *Summary Check-Off Form* (SCOF).
3. Illustrate by referring to a student's PFS and showing the class how this student would transfer information from this form to his/her SCOF. (See Instructional Tips.)

4. Tell the students to continue this procedure until they have checked off the Data–People–Things Environment, Ability, and Satisfaction categories for every job and leisure activity.

5. Remind teammates to help each other complete this activity.

6. Ask students to raise their hand if they need assistance.

7. After this activity, ask each team to conduct a discussion period.

Discussion

Ask a volunteer from each team to lead a discussion by asking the following questions:

- How did this exercise help you clarify your job and leisure preferences?
- Did you learn anything new about your job and leisure likes and dislikes?
- Are you more aware of your job or leisure activity interests? Why?
- Are you interested in learning more about your job or leisure choices? Why?
- Did anything about your job or leisure selections surprise you?

Appreciation (omit)

Instructional Tips

1. Be prepared to illustrate to the class how to check off the SCOF.

2. Refer to a student's PSF and show the class how he/she would transfer information to the SCOF as follows:
   - This student has selected computer programming.
   - This is a data job so the student would check off data.
   - This job usually takes place indoors in a city, so the student would check off "urban" and "indoors."
   - This job requires critical thinking and creativity so he/she would check off these categories.
   - Satisfactions from this job are earning good money and gaining independence, and these categories are checked off accordingly.

3. Remind the students to apply this illustration to other categories as well, such as People. If People is listed on a PSF, they would look for people-oriented jobs on their SCOF and proceed as illustrated above.

Anticipated Results

✓ The students understand how the categories on their PSF—Data—People–Things, Environment, Abilities, Satisfaction—correlate with their job and leisure activity choices.

✓ The students have completed checking off their SCOFs to ensure this understanding.

ACTIVITY 7

BECOMING KNOWLEDGEABLE ABOUT JOBS AND LEISURE ACTIVITIES

Purpose

For students to become knowledgeable about their top job and leisure activity choices.

Skill Development

The student will:

✓ learn important facts about his/her top jobs and leisure activity choices
✓ practice good communication skills through team discussion

Materials

- Copies of the *Occupational Outlook Handbook* and/or other career description resources
- *What I Learned About Jobs and Leisure Activities* form
- Completed copies of the *Summary Check-Off Form* (from activity 4)
- *Guidelines for Arranging and Conducting a Visitation* form

Introduction (2 minutes)

The leader will introduce this activity as follows:

1. Explain to the students that the purpose of this activity is to learn important facts about their job and leisure activity choices.

2. Inform them that through this process they will narrow their selections to a top job and leisure activity. The goal of this course is to get them involved in these activities.

Procedure (2 class periods)

The leader will conduct this activity as follows:

1. Ask the students to meet in their teams and bring their Summary Check-Off Forms (SCOFs).

2. Ask them to select one job and one leisure activity from each of their three career and leisure activity fields listed on their SCOFs.

3. Remind them that their chosen jobs and leisure activities will match with their Data–People–Things, Environment, Abilities, and Satisfaction selections.

4. Pass out copies of the What I Learned About Jobs and Leisure Activities Form to team members.

5. Show them how to record their three top jobs and leisure activities on this form.

6. Review this form by explaining how the terms in the evaluation sections relate to whether a job or leisure activity is rated good or poor and to answer questions accordingly. (See Instructional Tips for examples.)

7. Remind the students that they must get additional facts to complete this study by:

   • studying resources such as the *Occupational Outlook Handbook* and library resources

   • interviewing experts in the field (See *Guidelines for Arranging and Conducting a Visitation.*)

8. After completing this evaluation, ask the students to choose two top jobs and leisure activities. Record these selections on their forms as indicated in the directions.

9. After finishing this activity, students will meet in discussion groups to share their top selections with teammates.

Discussion (10 minutes)

1. Ask a volunteer from each team to lead a discussion by asking the following questions.

   • What new things did you learn about your top jobs and leisure activities?

   • Did you learn anything that discouraged you about getting involved in a specific job or leisure activity?

- What excites you the most about one of your job or leisure activity choices?

- How can you get involved in a job or leisure activity?

2. Ask students to share their thoughts about why they are considering replacing drug, gang, or other negative activities with a job or leisure activity choice.

Appreciation (omit)

Instructional Tips

1. Be sure that you have career description resources available for the students to study. Order instructional materials for the classroom and check with your career resource center or school library.

   - Organize a list of experts in the field, by career fields, and make arrangements for interviews. Have a plan for students to follow on conducting the interviewing process. See the Guidelines for Arranging and Conducting a Visitation form.

   - Be prepared to define the meaning of the terms listed on the What I Learned About Jobs and Leisure Activities form. For example, explain what a physical setting might be like on a specific job by using the following questions:

   - Will the employees interact with each other or work alone?

   - Is the job physically or mentally tiring?

   - Is the job performed in a clean or dirty environment?

   These kinds of considerations may make a difference in whether or not a student would be interested in a job.

2. For your information, the categories used for rating jobs was taken from the *Occupational Outlook Handbook*. A sample of the categories are:

   - working conditions

   - salary and benefits

   - interesting work

   - opportunity for advancement

   - job outlook

   - working hours

   - challenging work

   - training and education

Refer to the resource index at the back of this guide for an address in ordering copies of the *Occupational Outlook Handbook.*

Anticipated Results

The students have a thorough understanding of their job and leisure activity selections. Consequently, they have chosen their two top jobs and leisure activities.

Guidelines for Arranging and Conducting a Visitation

Below is a guide for arranging your visitation by phone. The main elements are the same should you make this contact in person.

✓ Speak clearly and slowly. Ask to speak to the contact person directly.

✓ Expect to make the appointment. Most people will be happy to help you for three main reasons: (1) you have been referred by someone they know, (2) you are a student seeking "real world" information, and (3) you have approached them in a businesslike manner.

✓ Give your name when calling, mention the name of the person who referred you, and state your business as briefly as possible.

Example: Say "This is (name) and I was referred to you by (name). As a part of my Career Assessment course at (school name), I have determined that the kind of work you do is of interest to me. If your schedule permits, I would like to make an appointment with you to find out more about the work you do and to help me make judgments about my career planning. When do you think you'd be able to give me about a half hour of your time to do this?

✓ Write down important information about the visitation, such as:

—Day, date, and time of appointment

—Place of appointment

—Name of person/persons to see (including the secretary's name)

✓ Conclude the phone conversation with a sincere *"thank you."* Learn to respect the value of other people's time.

(continued on next page)

Guidelines for Arranging
and Conducting a Visitation
(continued)

FINAL PREPARATIONS

As you approach the on-site visitation, be sure that you have attended to the items below. Ask your teacher and/or your parents for help if you are uncertain about any item.

On-Site Visitation Checklist

____ Dress appropriately for the work environment visited

____ Plan transportation (to and from)

____ Be slightly early for the appointment

____ Bring all necessary materials for the interview (see instructions for visit)

____ Obtain *advance approval* for use of a tape recorder and/or camera (optional)

____ Plan for a half-hour maximum (unless you are invited to stay longer for a tour of the facility, for example)

____ Get excited, enthusiastic, and plan on learning and having some fun

THE VISIT

Below is a checklist of the items you will need to complete your visitation:

____ Interview questionnaire

____ Two pens

____ Folder or binder

____ Tape recorder to record interview (optional)

____ Camera for pictures of people/work environment (optional)

____ Follow several simple rules for a successful interview. Remember you are not seeking a job, but information.

(continued on next page)

Guidelines for Arranging and Conducting a Visitation
(continued)

- Introduce yourself and shake hands.

- Allow the interviewer to select the meeting place and arrange details.

- Repeat the purpose of your visit briefly.

- Relax and just be yourself.

- Confirm that it is okay to tape the interview (if previously approved).

- Enjoy yourself and make this a tremendous learning experience.

- Pay attention to possible employment opportunities that may exist for you in this company or in the industry in general.

- Conclude with a "thank you" to all the people who will make your visit a memorable one.

- Send a short thank you note following your visit.

SUMMARY

Based upon the information gained from your on-site visitation, answer the following questions on a separate sheet of paper.

- What did you particularly like and/or dislike in this work environment?

- Were the contact person's daily activities and responsibilities what you expected? In what ways were they different?

- What unexpected, meaningful information did you gain?

- Do you feel that this occupation is related to your own interests, abilities, and personality?

- Do you feel you could be happy and successful in this occupation? Explain.

- What was the value of this on-site visitation in helping you learn more about this occupation?

WHAT I LEARNED ABOUT JOBS AND LEISURE ACTIVITIES FORM

Note: Think in terms of how a job and leisure activity can have a positive impact on yourself, friends, and family.

WHAT I LEARNED ABOUT JOBS

Rate Each Category As Follows: *3 = Good   2 = Fair   1 = Poor*

List Three Top Jobs	WORKING CONDITIONS	SALARY AND BENEFITS	INTERESTING WORK	OPPORTUNITY FOR ADVANCEMENT	JOB OUTLOOK	WORKING HOURS	CHALLENGING WORK	TRAINING AND EDUCATION	TOTAL POINTS
_____									
_____									
_____									

Review Completed Rating and Select the Two Top Jobs:

1._____   2._____

WHAT I LEARNED ABOUT LEISURE ACTIVITIES

Rate Each Category As Follows: *3 = Good   2 = Fair   1 = Poor*

List Three Leisure Activities	AFFORDABLE	CHALLENGING STIMULATING	INTERESTING ENTERTAINING	ACCESSIBLE	THOUGHT PROVOKING	COMPETITIVE	APPEALING ENVIRONMENT	ASSIST OTHERS	RELAXING	TOTAL POINTS
_____										
_____										
_____										

Review Completed Rating and Select the Two Top Leisure Activities:

1._____   2._____

ACTIVITY 8

SELECTING A TOP JOB
AND LEISURE ACTIVITY

Purpose

To understand how one's living conditions can affect the selection of a job or leisure activity.

Skill Development

The student will learn how to evaluate the facts needed to select a top job and leisure activity.

Materials

- *Relevant Facts Sheet*
- *What I Learned About Jobs and Leisure Activities* form (from activity 7)
- *A List of Community Resources* (see Instructional Tips)
- Pencils or pens

Introduction (1 minute)

The leader will introduce this activity as follows:

1. Explain to the students that today they will evaluate relevant factors that could affect their job or leisure activity selections. Through this process, they will arrive at a top job and leisure activity.

2. Remind the students that by participating in their top job and leisure activities, they can focus their time and energy on productive activities instead of negative activities that could cause discipline problems at school.

Procedure (35 minutes)

The leader will conduct this activity as follows:

1. Ask the students to meet in their teams and bring their *What I Learned About Jobs and Leisure Activities* forms with them.

RELEVANT FACTS SHEET

Student: _____   Date: _____

JOBS TO PURSUE

1. _____

2. _____

LOCATION OF SCHOOL, JOB, OR TRAINING

1. _____

2. _____

LEISURE ACTIVITIES TO PURSUE

1. _____

2. _____

LOCATION OF COMMUNITY RESOURCES

1. _____

2. _____

Review the following factors to determine how they can have a positive or negative effect on the selection of the above job or leisure activity choices. Choose the most realistic and desirable job and leisure activity.

1. *Family situation:* How will your relationship with your parents or relatives affect your job or leisure choices?

2. *Personal problems:* Do you have a drug, alcohol, health, or emotional problem? If the answer is yes, how could this problem affect your job or leisure activity selections?

3. *Housing and finances:* Will you be living at home, with relatives or friends, or living on your own? Will you need income for rent, food, clothing, and transportation?

(continued on next page)

4. *Transportation:* Do you have a driver's license and access to a car? How do you plan to get to a job, school, or training?

5. *Vocational skills and work experience:* What skills and experience do you have that will qualify you for a job? Will you need to develop or upgrade your skills to qualify for a good job?

6. *Leisure activity skills:* What leisure activity skills do you now possess? Will you need to develop or upgrade your leisure skills to your level of satisfaction?

7. *Educational background:* Do you have a high school diploma or GED? Will you need a graduation diploma to qualify for your career choice?

8. *Age and marital status:* Are you 18, married, or single? Will you need to be 18 years old to qualify for the school, job, or training desired?

After weighing the above facts, the following job and leisure activity choices appear to be the most realistic.

Job Selection: Leisure Activity Selection:

_____   _____

2. Pass out copies of the *Relevant Facts Sheet* to all students.

3. Refer students to a *List of Community Resources* (see Instructional Tips).

4. Instruct the students in how to record their two top jobs and leisure activities with the names of:

   • an employer or supervisor

   • a school or recreation program

   • a vocational training program or a community member

   This information is printed under the appropriate headings on the Relevant Facts Sheet.

5. Instruct the students in how to complete sections one to eight of this form. Refer to Instructional Tips for additional directions.

6. Ask teammates to help each other or work in pairs to weigh the relevant factors, and arrive at answers to the questions covering these factors.

7. Remind the students to record pertinent notes after each question as they complete their Relevant Facts Sheet.

8. After weighing these factors, ask the students to select and record a top job and leisure activity.

9. Move from team to team and assist as needed.

10. After completing this activity, students will meet in their teams to share their top jobs and leisure activity selections.

Discussion (20 minutes)

(**Note:** this discussion period will take a second class period)

Ask a volunteer from each team to lead a discussion by asking the following questions:

• Were there any problems that you had a difficult time dealing with? Explain.

• Does anyone have any suggestions that would help?

• Did anyone ever have to deal with this type of problem before?

• Does anyone have any problems they would like help with?

• Which items were the toughest to deal with? Why?

• Does anyone have some ideas on how to deal with this problem?

Appreciation (omit)

Instructional Tips:

Note: In preparation for this activity, the teacher will have a List of Community Resources that includes:

- vocational schools or programs
- community agencies and recreation programs
- local colleges
- community members with special expertise
- local business and industry

This list would include the names of contact people and the addresses of these community facilities. The school counselor should have access to this information and assist the teacher accordingly.

1. Using this list, provide each student with the appropriate resources for his/her job and leisure selection.
2. Remind the students that deciding where to go for work, training, or a leisure activity has an important bearing on their selection process.
3. Before beginning this activity, stress the fact that students must be realistic in what they can accomplish, and they must think in terms of their real-life circumstances. For example, have them consider the following factors:
   - personal problems
   - housing and finances
   - transportation
   - vocational skills
   - educational background

   Ask them to bounce ideas off a teammate, and remind them that they will have an opportunity to get advice from teammates during a discussion period.

Anticipated Results

The students understand the relevant factors that can enhance or deter their job selection process. Consequently, they are able to successfully select a top job and leisure activity.

ACTIVITY 9

COMPLETING JOB AND LEISURE
ACTIVITY ACTION PLANS

Purpose

To understand how to compete a job and leisure action plan.

Skill Development

The student will learn how to:

✓ complete Job and Leisure Activity Action Plans

✓ practice good communication skills as a member of a discussion group

Materials

- *Completed Relevant Facts Sheets* (from activity 8)
- *Job Action Plan forms*
- *Leisure Activity Action Plan*
- Pencils or pens

Introduction (1 minute)

The leader will introduce this activity as follows:

1. Inform the students that today they will complete their Job and Leisure Activity Action Plans.

2. Tell them that their plans will give them the directions they need to get started in their job and leisure activity selections.

3. Remind the students that they are expected to spend their time and energy in getting and keeping a job or participating in a leisure activity, not on negative activities.

Procedure (2 class periods)

The leader will conduct this activity as follows:

1. Ask the students to meet in their teams and to bring their *Relevant Facts Sheet* with them.

JOB ACTION PLAN

NAME_____ DATE_____

JOB GOAL _____

List vocational training, education, classes to take, career exploration, and/or work experience, and any other activities necessary to reach my goal:

_____

_____

_____

_____

Where will I go to get the vocational training, education, exploratory and/or work experience, or on-the-job training?

_____

_____

When will I begin my education, vocational training, exploratory and/or work experience, or on-the-job training?

_____

How will I begin and what steps will I need to take to reach my job goal?

_____

_____

_____

Possible barriers that might prevent me from reaching my job goal:

_____

_____

_____

Ways to deal with these barriers:

_____

_____

_____

Deadline for reaching my job goal:

_____

2. Pass out copies of the *Job and Leisure Activity Action Plans* to all students.

3. Review these action plans with the students and answer their questions.

4. Ask the students to complete their action plans and to get help from you or a teammate if necessary.

5. Move from team to team and help as needed.

6. Remind the students that if they need additional help, they will get assistance during the team sharing period.

7. Use the first class period for the students to complete their Action Plans.

8. During the second class period, ask the students to conduct a sharing session in light of the following questions. Ask for a team leader to facilitate this activity.

   - Did you have any difficulty completing any part of your Action Plans? Explain. Does anyone have any suggestions to help (name)?

   - Which sections were the most difficult to complete? Why? Does anyone have any helpful ideas or suggestions?

   - Do you need any help to improve your plans? How? Who can help (name)? Any ideas?

Instructional Tips

1. Take the time to answer questions before students begin working on their plans.

2. Remind the students to refer to their Relevant Facts Sheets for information about where to go for education, training, and so on.

3. Move from team to team and monitor discussion groups, and provide input as needed.

4. Follow up periodically to be sure students are implementing their plans via progress review meetings. Refer to the deadline date on the action plans to schedule these meetings.

5. It is recommended that the counselor assist the teacher to implement an after-school program. Most counselors are familiar with and have access to community resources. Therefore, to form a community network of resources the following steps are recommended:

   - Organize a list of community organizations and members that are logical resources for career and leisure activities.

   - Contact these community members to secure their support in providing career and leisure activities for at-risk students. Explain the importance of this program.

   - Organize a meeting with the community agencies and members that are interested in supporting this program to:

LEISURE ACTIVITY ACTION PLAN

NAME_____   DATE_____

LEISURE GOAL _____

List educational training necessary to reach my goal:

_____

_____

Where will I go to get this education and/or training:

_____

_____

When will I begin this education and/or training:

_____

How will I begin and what steps will I take to reach my leisure goal:

_____

_____

_____

Possible barriers that might prevent me from reaching my goal:

_____

_____

_____

Ways to deal with these barriers:

_____

_____

_____

Deadline for reaching my leisure goal:

_____

✓ discuss the importance of getting our youth off the streets and into productive activities

✓ develop a referral system with the contact people representing the school and the representative agencies to create a supportive working relationship

✓ provide agency members with an awareness of other available resources for youths so they can refer them to appropriate services as needed

✓ organize a network of agencies and community members by exchanging addresses, phone numbers, and names of contact people. A list of these community members with all pertinent information should be given to every network member.

Anticipated Results

✓ The students understand how to complete their action plan.

✓ Students will use their action plans as a guide to obtain a job or begin a leisure activity.

✓ Students have stopped bringing drugs, guns, or other gang-related problems to school, which has eliminated discipline problems in the classroom.

PARENT SUPPORT PROGRAM

INTRODUCTION

Section 5 is designed to provide a parent support program to augment the Collaborative Discipline Process. The teacher and counselor identify students with discipline problems in the classroom. They then contact the parents of these students in order to meet with them and their children. The goal of this meeting is to get the support of the parents in helping their children eliminate discipline problems in the classroom. The teacher and/or counselor, parents, and students collaborate to arrive at a behavioral contract that will accomplish the following:

- change negative behavior to positive behavior in the classroom
- eliminate discipline problems from occurring in the classroom

For specifics on how to complete the behavioral contract, refer to Step 1 of the Discipline Prevention Program "Understanding Each Student's Behavioral Problems" in Section 1, *Bonding*. Refer to the Behavioral Contract form at the end of this introduction.

At the conclusion of the above meeting, the student, parents, teacher, and counselor will agree to a long-range behavioral goal. Since the purpose of this behavioral goal is for the student to eliminate discipline problems so that he/she can succeed in school, the student, teacher, counselor, and parent will agree to an annual long-range academic goal. This academic goal is dependent upon the student meeting his/her behavioral goal. Changing negative behavior to positive behavior is crucial towards eliminating discipline problems and meeting the long-range educational goal.

To successfully change the negative behavior of at-risk students in school, it is very important that the parents understand why their children are misbehaving. Parental input, understanding, and agreement to the terms of their child's contract is imperative. If the parents don't acknowledge or agree with the terms of the contract, they are less apt to support their child in the implementation of the contract. Accordingly, this meeting is mandatory for parents of at-risk students with discipline problems. Parents attend this meeting in September before instruction begins in the classroom, as the terms of the behavioral contract should begin on the first day of classroom instruction. An ideal arrangement is to conduct the parent meetings in conjunction with the bonding activities during the first two weeks of school. Refer to the suggested two-week schedule described in "Implementing Student Support Teams" found in the beginning of the book.

It is very important that the teacher and/or counselor convince the parents that their support in helping their child to change his/her negative behavior is

201

crucial towards their child succeeding in school. Consequently, the teacher and counselor must develop an outstanding rapport with the parents. They must convey to the parents that they sincerely care about their child and will try their best to help their child succeed in school. However, the parents must understand that they play an important role in working with the teacher, counselor, and their child to remedy discipline problems in the classroom. Accordingly, the teacher must inform the parents that through a series of parent seminars, they can learn the communication and critical thinking skills necessary to prepare them for helping their child change his/her negative behavior. Explain that through this collaborative effort the parents, teacher, counselor, and student can work together to quell discipline problems in the classroom. Through this personalized approach, the teacher and counselor can "sell" the parents on attending the parent seminars. As a follow-up to this meeting, the teacher and/or counselor will phone the parents and invite them to attend the parent seminars. Through this approach, as compared with just making a phone call or sending a letter, over 70% to 80% of the parents have attended parent seminars in this program.

In conjunction with learning communication and critical thinking skills, parents become a support group. They understand that other parents' children have the same discipline problems that their child has and console, support, and advise each other accordingly. When conducting a support group meeting, on an informal basis, allow the parents to discuss the discipline problems that their children are having at school or at home. Ask the question: "Does anyone have a discipline problem with his/her child that he/she would like to share with our group?" This question generally stimulates a discussion. The discussion can lead to helpful tips from the parents, teacher, or counselor. The discussion can also lead into a specific activity in the parent seminar that prepares the parents for coping with a specific discipline problem. The leader should facilitate this discussion by asking good open-ended questions and using reflective listening techniques.

As members of the support team, the parents must meet with the teacher, counselor, and their child when their child fails to abide by the terms of his/her behavioral contract. Accordingly, they will review and revise the behavioral contract, as needed. Through a collaborative discipline process, the student support team members will assist the teacher in monitoring the student's behavioral progress in the classroom. In addition, the parents will support their child through school meetings, as described above, and by ensuring that their child practices "like" behavior at home. Through this Collaborative Discipline Process the parents, teacher, counselor, student support team, and student work collaboratively to eliminate discipline problems in the classroom.

Each parent seminar lasts 2½ hours. Sessions include two to three activities which allows parents time to share on an informal basis as a support group. A good time span is from 7:00 PM to 9:30 PM. It is recommended to take a fifteen minute refreshment break to serve coffee and cookies, and so on midway through the seminar. This break adds variety to the seminar and gives the parents an opportunity to socialize on an informal basis. The parent seminars meet weekly over a seven week period. However, many parents are interested in continuing the informal support group meetings after the formalized sessions have concluded; the teacher and/or counselor can continue these meetings every other week or once monthly. An outline of the seminar sessions are as follows:

SESSION I

> **Activity 1,** Getting to Know Each Other and Becoming Familiar with the Program
>
> **Activity 2,** Sharing Personal Interests with Other Parents

SESSION II

> **Activity 3,** Building a Comfortable, Supportive, and Disciplined Family Environment
>
> **Activity 4,** Agreeing on Ground Rules
>
> *Conduct a parent support group meeting.*

SESSION III

> **Activity 5,** Learning and Practicing Conversation Skills
>
> **Activity 6,** Learning and Practicing Good Listening Skills
>
> *Conduct a parent support group meeting.*

SESSION IV

> **Activity 7,** Recognizing and Avoiding Poor Listening Habits
>
> **Activity 8,** Learning How to Observe Others
>
> **Activity 9,** Learning How to Empathize with Others

SESSION V

> **Activity 10,** Learning How to Make I-Feel Statements
>
> **Activity 11,** Learning How to Say I-Feel Statements
>
> *Conduct a parent support group meeting.*

SESSION VI

> **Activity 12,** Defining and Clarifying a Problem
>
> **Activity 13,** Arriving at and Evaluating an Alternative Solution
>
> **Activity 14,** Making and Implementing a Decision

SESSION VII

> **Activity 15,** Learning Important Facts About Alcohol and Other Drugs

Another possibility is for the students and parents to practice the communication and critical thinking skills in unison through an advanced seminar series at school. To prepare for these seminars, it is recommended that the parents and their children have completed the basic activities as described in Sections I, II, III, and IV. An experienced counselor who is educated and trained to work with families should be selected for this assignment. Furthermore, the readiness for the family to engage in the seminars must be carefully evaluated by professionals in the field.

During the initial parent meeting, the long-range academic and behavioral goals are recorded on the *Long-Range Educational Goals* form. (See the following page.) Also on this form there are spaces for vocational and leisure activity goals. The vocational and leisure activity goals are arrived at and recorded on this form during participation in Section IV. All goals are to be achieved by the end of the current school year.

LONG-RANGE EDUCATIONAL GOALS

NAME _____   DATE _____

TEACHER _____   SCHOOL _____

ACADEMIC LONG-RANGE GOAL:

_____

_____

BEHAVIORAL LONG-RANGE GOAL:

_____

_____

VOCATIONAL LONG-RANGE GOAL:

_____

_____

LEISURE ACTIVITY LONG-RANGE GOAL:

_____

_____

The following team members agree that _____
should pursue the above educational goals.

Teacher _____   Counselor _____
         signature   signature

Student _____   Parent _____
         signature   signature

SCHEDULE OF PARENT SEMINARS

SESSION I

    Activity 1, Getting to Know Each Other and Becoming Familiar with the Program

    Activity 2, Sharing Personal Interests with Other Parents

SESSION II

    Activity 3, Building a Comfortable, Supportive, and Disciplined Family Environment

    Activity 4, Agreeing on Ground Rules

    Conduct a parent support group meeting.

SESSION III

    Activity 5, Learning and Practicing Conversation Skills

    Activity 6, Learning and Practicing Good Listening Skills

    Conduct a parent support group meeting.

SESSION IV

    Activity 7, Recognizing and Avoiding Poor Listening Habits

    Activity 8, Learning How to Observe Others

    Activity 9, Learning How to Empathize with Others

SESSION V

    Activity 10, Learning How to Make I-Feel Statements

    Activity 11, Learning How to Say I-Feel Statements

    Conduct a parent support group meeting.

SESSION VI

    Activity 12, Defining and Clarifying a Problem

    Activity 13, Arriving at and Evaluating an Alternative Solution

    Activity 14, Making and Implementing a Decision

SESSION VII

    Activity 15, Learning Important Facts About Alcohol and Other Drugs

BEHAVIORAL CONTRACT

NAME _____ DATE _____

TARGET BEHAVIOR: (Replace negative behavior with positive behavior)

NEGATIVE BEHAVIOR: _____

_____

_____

_____

POSITIVE BEHAVIOR: _____

_____

_____

_____

_____ AGREES TO:
(student's name)

1. _____

2. _____

3. _____

4. _____

5. _____

PROGRESS REVIEW MEETING DATE:_____

BONUS FOR MEETING BEHAVIORAL GOAL: _____

_____

PENALTY FOR NOT MEETING GOAL: _____

_____

WE UNDERSTAND AND AGREE TO THE TERMS OF THIS CONTRACT.

_____ _____   _____ _____
student's signature   (date)   teacher's signature   (date)

_____ _____   _____ _____
parent's signature   (date)   counselor's signature   (date)

SESSION I—ACTIVITY 1

GETTING TO KNOW OTHERS
AND BECOMING FAMILIAR WITH THE PROGRAM

Purpose

To gain an understanding of the parent seminars and meet other people.

Skill Development

The parents will learn:

✓ a technique for introducing themselves to others
✓ new and interesting things about the names of other parents

Materials

Schedule of Parent Seminars handout.

Introduction (10 minutes)

The leader will introduce this activity as follows.

1. Explain to the parents that through the seminars they will learn the same communication and critical-thinking skills that are being taught to their children. Thus, they can practice these skills at home with their children to:
   - improve communication skills
   - help family members cope with personal or family problems
   - reinforce discipline at home and at school
2. Refer to the schedule of the parent seminars and briefly describe the program.
3. Remind the parents that a goal of the parent seminars is to prepare them in how to help their children overcome discipline problems in the classroom and at home.

Procedure (35 minutes)

The leader will conduct this activity as follows.

1. Seat the parents in a full circle.

2. Pass out copies of the Schedule of Parent Seminars and Review the schedule with parents.

3. Explain that they will introduce themselves to the group by giving their full name, the origin of their name by nationality, and anything else interesting or unusual about their name, such as:

   • who you were named after

   • a funny story about your name

   • a nickname

   • any feelings about the significance of your name

4. Begin by using these guidelines to introduce yourself to the group.

5. Call on someone else, at random, to introduce him/herself to the group.

6. Follow this process until everyone has had a chance to introduce themselves to the group.

7. Remind everyone to pay close attention and make every effort to remember as many names as possible.

Discussion (10 minutes)

Explain to the parents that we usually follow each activity with a discussion to enhance an understanding of what has been learned. Lead a discussion by asking the following questions:

   • How did this activity help you to get to know the other parents better?

   • How did you feel about introducing yourself to the group?

   • Following your introduction, how did you decide who to pick for the next introduction?

   • Did you learn anything new or interesting about any of the parents' names?

Appreciation (10 minutes)

   ✓ Explain to the parents that when time permits we end an activity by saying something positive about someone in our group. Tell them that we use this appreciation period to enhance the self-esteem of their children.

   ✓ Ask the parents to say something positive about what someone did or said in their group. Begin by saying something positive about one of the parents.

Instructional Tips

1. Take the time to review the seminar schedule and stress the importance of their participation in these activities. Answer questions accordingly.

2. Role model the introduction of yourself to create a comfortable feeling among the parents.

3. Explain that after they introduce themselves, they will select someone else at random to make the next introduction.

4. Use effective open-ended questions and reflective listening techniques during the discussion period.

5. Remind the parents that their children follow this same process during their activity periods

6. When working with parents with a limited ability to speak English, it is recommended there be an assistant or a parent who speaks the native language to act as an interpreter. Ideally, a teacher or counselor who speaks the native language of the parents, such as Spanish, should lead the seminar activities. Also, special English laboratories can be organized by the school district to teach the parents survival English. Through this approach, the parents can prepare themselves to participate in English-speaking school activities, and so forth.

Anticipated Results

✓ The parents understand that the purpose of the seminar activities is to learn the positive communication and critical thinking skills necessary to prepare them for helping their children overcome discipline problems in school and at home.

✓ The parents become acquainted with each other.

SESSION I—ACTIVITY 2

SHARING PERSONAL INTERESTS WITH OTHER PARENTS

Purpose

To become better acquainted with the other parents.

Skill Development

The parents will learn how to:

✓ share personal interests with others

✓ follow directions in an action-oriented activity

✓ focus on a task to complete an activity

Materials

- Two sets of 5 x 8 cards with different colored dots (see Instructional Tips)
- Pens or pencils
- A chart illustrating a sample card
- A list of questions for conducting the discussion

Introduction (5 minutes)

The leader will introduce this activity as follows:

1. Seat the parents in a full circle.
2. Tell them that they will continue with another community building activity to become better acquainted with the other parents.
3. Ask the parents to take turns saying their names along with an adjective that describes how they feel tonight.
4. Begin by role modeling this activity by sharing information with another parent.
5. Ask the person to your left to continue this activity and then proceed around the circle.
6. Tell the parents that their children have participated in this same activity to promote bonding among the students and the teacher and/or counselor.
7. Explain that bonding is the first step in building trust and respect among the students and the teacher, and that when students trust and respect each other they are less apt to incur discipline problems in the classroom.

Procedure (35 minutes)

The leader will conduct this activity as follows:

1. Distribute the cards with different colored dots evenly among the parents to form separate groups.
2. Ask the parents to print their names just above the dot with an adjective describing the kind of person they are just below the dot (refer to the sample card).
3. Refer to the sample card illustration and tell the parents to print the following information:

- two things they can do well at the bottom of their cards
- a favorite place to visit at the top of their cards
- a favorite food on the right side of their cards
- their favorite car or music on the left side of their cards

4. Do this activity with the parents.

5. Ask the parents to get up from their chairs and move around the room to find a parent with the same colored dot and introduce themselves to each other.

6. Tell the parents to begin by saying something about their descriptive adjective.

7. Give the parents enough time to cover the topic and then ask them to find another parent with the same colored dot and discuss two things that they can do well.

8. Follow the same rotation while discussing the other parts of the card.

Discussion (10 minutes)

Depending upon the size of the group, have them meet in two groups (by the color of their dots) or meet as one group. Lead a discussion by asking the following questions:

- How did it feel to share with others?
- Did you find any similarities in the things you like to do? Explain.
- Did you learn anything new that impressed or surprised you about another parent?

Appreciation (5 minutes)

Ask each parent to say something positive about what another parent did or said tonight.

Instructional Tips

1. This activity is identical to activity 2 in Section I. Refer to this activity to get specific directions on how to prepare dotted cards and conduct this activity.

2. In preparation for this activity, draw or reproduce the same card that is illustrated in Section I.

3. If the number of parents is large, get a fellow teacher or counselor to assist you with activities in the seminar series. Ideally, a counselor should team with you to assist with the parent and study activities.

4. To become better acquainted with the parents, you should do this activity with them.

5. Participation in this activity will help you control the time spent on this activity.

6. Refer to the Instructional Tips in Section I, activity 2.

Anticipated Results

✓ The parents and the teacher or school staff are becoming better acquainted with each other by sharing personal interests and initiating friendships with each other. They are bonding as a group.

✓ They understand that their children are building trust and respect among each other in the classroom through participation in this activity. Consequently, their children are less apt to get into discipline problems.

SESSION II—ACTIVITY 3

BUILDING A COMFORTABLE, SUPPORTIVE, AND DISCIPLINED FAMILY ENVIRONMENT

Purpose

To become aware of what makes a family environment comfortable or uncomfortable.

Skill Development

The parents will learn how to:

✓ share and express experiences, opinions, and beliefs with others

✓ accept and respect the different beliefs of others

✓ work cooperatively with others in a brainstorming session

Materials

• A paper pad on which to print statements
• Marking pens

Introduction (5 minutes)

The leader will introduce this activity as follows:

1. Explain to the parents that when they interact with their child or family members, it is important that everyone get along well.

2. Tell them that the purpose of this activity is to help them build a supportive and comfortable family environment where family members assist each other in times of need.

3. Ask the parents to share with the group how they have built a supportive environment in their home. Encourage them to share their experiences and ideas.

4. Inform them to share their feelings and opinions as openly and honestly as possible.

5. Explain that feeling comfortable or uncomfortable in their home will depend upon how family members treat each other. For example, if family members tease each other, put each other down, don't listen to each other, or gossip about each other, they will not have mutual feelings of trust and respect.

6. Inform the parents that their children have used this activity to arrive at expected behavior in the classroom. By practicing this activity with their children at home, their children will have the guidelines needed to practice positive behavior in the family environment.

7. Remind the parents to stress to their children the need to behave in a positive manner at school as well as at home in order to eliminate discipline problems. **Note:** This focus on positive behavior in school reinforces their child's need to adhere to the terms of his/her behavioral contract.

Procedure

The leader will conduct this activity as follows:

1. If the group is composed of 20 or more parents, divide them into two groups.

2. Ask for a volunteer(s) to act as recorders, and ask the recorders to list the headings "comfortable" and "uncomfortable" on a paper pad.

3. Ask each group to brainstorm what makes them feel comfortable in their relationships with family members.

4. Ask the recorders to record these ideas under the "comfortable" heading.

5. Next, ask them to brainstorm what makes them feel uncomfortable in their relationships with family members.

6. Under the "uncomfortable" heading, ask them to think in terms of situations that erupt into discipline problems between parents and their children.

7. Ask the recorders to record these items.

8. Add items to the lists as appropriate.

Discussion (omit)

Appreciation (omit)

Instructional Tips

Refer to the instructional tips for the same activity for students in Section I, activity 4.

Anticipated Results

✓ The parents understand why it is important to build a positive family environment, and they have arrived at a list of items that make family members feel either comfortable or uncomfortable in the family setting.

✓ Parents understand how the uncomfortable items relate to discipline problems at home, and understand how practicing positive behavior in the home reinforces their child's practicing of positive behavior at school.

SESSION II—ACTIVITY 4

AGREEING ON GROUND RULES

Purpose

To agree on a set of ground rules for the family to abide by.

Skill Development

The parents will learn how to:

✓ combine and eliminate statements that are similar or repetitive and compile a list of acceptable ground rules

✓ prioritize the most important statements to arrive at a set of ground rules

✓ practice working cooperatively as a group by accepting and respecting others' ideas, opinions, and beliefs.

Materials

- Paper pad
- Marking pens
- A list of questions for conducting the discussion

Introduction (3 minutes)

The leader will introduce this activity as follows:

1. Explain to the parents that tonight they will review their lists of comfortable and uncomfortable items, and select the most important items to form a set of ground rules.

2. Explain that these ground rules will provide guidelines that family members can use to provide positive support to each other at home.

3. Inform the parents that their children have experienced this activity at school to arrive at a behavioral code for standards of behavior in the classroom, and that by practicing positive behavior their children are less apt to get into discipline problems. **Note:** Hand out copies of the Behavioral Code to parents so they can have a "firsthand" perspective of what the code means. (See example in Section I.)

4. Remind them that by establishing ground rules at home, their children will be practicing positive behavior that can reinforce positive behavior at school.

5. Stress the point that through this activity the parents, teacher, counselor, and students are collaborating to arrive at positive behavior to replace negative behavior and deter discipline problems in the classroom.

Procedure (35 minutes)

The leader will conduct this activity as follows:

1. Ask the parents to meet in the same groups.

2. Ask them to review their lists of comfortable and uncomfortable items, and select the four most important items necessary to formulate a set of ground rules.

3. Give each parent an opportunity to give their reasons why an item is the most important to them.

4. After this discussion take a hand vote to arrive at the four most important items.

5. Remind the recorder to record the number of votes after each item on the list.

6. If the group cannot agree on four items, number the items under each heading and ask the parents to record the numbers of their four top choices on pieces of paper. Ask a parent to help you tally the vote.

7. Tell the parents to meet back in a full circle to review each group's list of four items and combine and/or eliminate items that are similar or repetitive.

8. Form a list of ground rules.

9. Remind the parents that the list of ground rules is used as a basis for establishing standards of discipline at home, and they will have to arrive at consequences for not abiding by the ground rules. Refer to activity 5 in Section I.

Discussion (omit)

Appreciation (omit)

Instructional Tips

Note: In this activity the parents will share their beliefs and opinions to arrive at a common list of ground rules, and they will understand how this process works. When doing this exercise with their families, they will establish specific ground rules that are relevant to their family.

Refer to the Instructional Tips and other information regarding a similar activity for the students in Section I, activity 5.

Anticipated Results

✓ The parents understand the value of abiding by ground rules when building a positive family environment, and have successfully developed a set of rules.

✓ Parents understand how the establishment of a behavioral code at school and ground rules at home will reinforce positive behavior in both environments, to deter discipline problems.

SESSION III—ACTIVITY 5

LEARNING AND PRACTICING CONVERSATION SKILLS

Purpose

To become knowledgeable in starting a conversation with a son or daughter.

Skill Development

The parents will learn how to:

✓ use techniques necessary to start a conversation

✓ ask open-ended questions

Materials

- Chart illustrating open- and closed-ended questions (from Section II, activity 2)
- Handout listing guidelines for starting a conversation (from Section II, activity 2)

Introduction (5 minutes)

The leader will introduce this activity as follows:

1. Tell the parents that tonight they will learn and practice how to start a conversation.
2. Refer briefly to the outline that lists the techniques to be covered in this activity.
3. Remind the parents that it is normal to have difficulty in communicating with teenagers, and a goal of this activity is to help them to start and sustain a conversation with their child.
4. Remind them that their child has learned and practiced these same communication techniques. One of the goals of this program is for them to practice the techniques at home with their children.
5. Remind parents that discipline problems result because of a lack of meaningful conversation between parents and children, and a goal of this activity is to improve conversation skills.

Procedure (35 minutes)

The leader will conduct this activity as follows:

1. Ask the parents to meet in a full circle.
2. Pass out copies of the Guidelines for Starting a Conversation.
3. Refer to the chart and illustrate the difference between an open-ended and a closed-ended question, and review the "Tips" for starting a conversation.
4. Illustrate how to start a conversation by role modeling an activity with a parent.
5. Start a conversation with your partner by asking about his or her interests. Pretend that he/she is your son or daughter and ask a question like: What happened today at basketball practice?
6. Follow up this question with another question that is related specifically to the answer, such as: Why do you believe your team is well prepared for the Central High game?
7. After two minutes have elapsed, stop and ask the group to critique the role-practicing activity.

8. Acknowledge the parents' response and ask appropriate open-ended questions to enhance an understanding of how to begin and sustain a conversation.

9. Ask the parents to pair off with the person to their left and take turns starting a conversation by asking open-ended questions.

10. After two minutes ask the parents to switch roles.

Discussion (omit)

Appreciation (omit)

Instructional Tips

1. Remind the parents that rebellion is a typical stage that most teenagers go through. They are striving to become independent from their parents, and want to make their own decisions. They may have the physical features of an adult, but still the questionable maturity of a teenager. They may think they have all the right answers. Many parents do not understand this and believe that their child has a bad attitude. When coupled with the problems of at-risk youth, parents can have a very difficult time communicating with their children.

2. Refer to the guidelines for starting a conversation and stress some of the positive ways to approach a child, such as:

   • complimenting them on looking nice or doing something well

   • speaking in a very sincere manner with a pleasant tone of voice

   • smiling and communicating in a friendly way

   • being a good listener and not interrupting your child

3. Assure the parents that if they put forth a good effort by using these guidelines, they will have an excellent opportunity to converse well with their child.

4. Refer to activity 2, Section II, to review Instructional Tips for the same activity along with *Guidelines for Starting a Conversation*.

Anticipated Results

✓ Parents understand how to start a conversation and feel comfortable about conversing with their son or daughter.

✓ They understand the importance of conducting meaningful conversations with their children to prevent discipline problems from occurring between them.

SESSION III—ACTIVITY 6

LEARNING AND PRACTICING GOOD LISTENING SKILLS

Purpose

To understand the skills that are necessary to be a good listener.

Skill Development

The parents will learn how to:

✓ make good eye contact

✓ listen carefully to the content and feelings behind a message

✓ use reflective listening techniques

✓ practice asking good open-ended questions

Materials

Three Steps to Good Listening Skills handout (from Section II, activity 3)

Introduction (5 minutes)

The leader will introduce this activity as follows:

1. Explain to the parents that good listening skills complement the asking of open-ended questions.

2. Remind them that a common fault of most parents is that they are poor listeners since they tend to do most of the talking through an authoritarian role. This is particularly true when parents are frustrated or angry.

3. Stress the need to relax and make an effort to listen to what their child has to say, and they will begin to understand where their child is "coming from."

4. Stress the fact that being a good listener is one of the most important communication skills in developing a rapport with their child.

5. Refer to the outline and review the good listening skills briefly.

6. Remind parents that discipline problems can arise when they refuse to listen to their child's "point of view" and anger erupts.

7. Inform them that their child has experienced this activity at school, and they should practice conversation and good listening skills at home with their child.

Procedure (30 minutes)

The leader will conduct this activity as follows.

1. Pass out and review copies of the Three Steps to Good Listening handout
2. Role practice good listening skills with a parent.
3. Ask the parent to tell you about something he or she admires a great deal, such as a friend, relative, or famous person, or a pet or favorite possession.
4. Converse for three minutes and then ask the group the following questions:
   - Which good listening skills did you observe?
   - How effective were the skills used?
5. Respond to the parents' answers and stress the key points important to good listening.
6. Ask parents to pair off with the person to their right and take turns practicing good listening skills using the same topic demonstrated by the leader.
7. After three minutes, ask the pairs to switch roles.
8. Move around the room and observe and assist as needed.

Discussion (10 minutes)

Lead the parents in a discussion by asking the following questions:

- Which role was the most difficult and why?
- How did it feel to be listened to? Explain.
- Which good listening skills were the most effective? Explain.
- How will these good listening skills help you to communicate with your son or daughter effectively?

Appreciation (5 minutes)

Ask the parents to say one positive thing that their partner did or said during the activity.

Instructional Tips

1. Remind the parents that it is very important to their child that they understand his/her feelings and concerns.
2. Stress the fact that they can be in tune with their child's feelings and concerns by:
   - listening carefully to the feelings and content behind a message

- acknowledging that they understand these feelings and concerns via reflective listening techniques
- asking appropriate follow-up questions that provide an open-ended response

3. Refer to Section II, activity 3 for Instructional Tips and guidelines for good listening.

Anticipated Results

✓ The parents understand how to be effective listeners and they exhibit their ability to practice good listening skills during a conversation.

✓ Parents understand the importance of listening to the concerns of their child and acknowledging the feelings behind the message, to prevent discipline problems from occurring at home.

SESSION IV—ACTIVITY 7

RECOGNIZING AND AVOIDING POOR LISTENING SKILLS

Purpose

To understand, identify, and avoid poor listening skills.

Skill Development

The parents will learn how to identify and avoid poor nonverbal and verbal listening skills.

Materials

- Poor Listening Skills handout (from Section II, activity 4)

Introduction (3 minutes)

The leader will introduce this activity as follows:

1. Explain to the parents that tonight they will learn how to recognize and avoid poor listening skills.

2. Remind them that poor listening habits break down a good conversation which makes it very difficult to communicate with others (including their children).

3. Tell the parents that poor listening skills can be verbal or nonverbal. (Refer to the handout listing poor listening habits.)

4. Stress the fact that they must try to eliminate poor listening habits and develop good listening skills in order to communicate with their son or daughter effectively.

5. Remind parents that using poor listening habits will convey the message that they are not interested in what their child has to say. Consequently, their child can become frustrated or angry and discipline problems can evolve.

6. Inform the parents that their child has experienced this activity at school. Thus, they can practice avoiding poor listening habits during conversations at home.

Procedure (30 minutes)

The leader will conduct this activity as follows:

1. Ask the parents to sit in a full circle.

2. Pass out and review the Poor Listening Skills handout.

3. Role practice the role of the listener and ask a parent to be the speaker.

4. Ask the speaker to tell you about a favorite place he/she likes to go on a weekend or for a vacation.

5. During this conversation demonstrate verbal and nonverbal poor listening habits.

6. Continue role practicing for two minutes.

7. Ask the parents to critique this demonstration by asking them the following questions: "Which poor listening habits offended you the most? Why?"

8. After a brief discussion, pair off the parents and ask them to role practice this same activity.

9. Move around the room and assist as needed.

10. After two minutes, ask the partners to switch roles.

Discussion (omit)

Appreciation (omit)

Instructional Tips

Refer to the list of nonverbal and verbal habits and the Instructional Tips in Section II, activity 4.

Anticipated Results

✓ The parents understand how to identify and avoid poor listening habits, and how to replace them with good listening skills in order to conduct a thoughtful conversation.

✓ They understand the importance of avoiding poor listening habits to prevent discipline problems from occurring between themselves and their children.

SESSION IV—ACTIVITY 8

LEARNING HOW TO OBSERVE OTHERS

Purpose

To understand how to observe and interpret the meaning of verbal and nonverbal communication.

Skill Development

The parents will learn how to observe and interpret verbal and nonverbal patterns of communication.

Materials

- Verbal and Nonverbal Styles of Communication handout (from Section II, activity 5)
- Paper pad and marking pens

Introduction (3 minutes)

The leader will introduce this activity as follows:

1. Explain to the parents that tonight they will learn how to interpret the meaning of verbal and nonverbal behavior by observing how people communicate with each other.

2. Remind them certain cues will tell them the mood of the other person, such as tone of voice, arm or hand gestures, facial expressions, and posture.

3. Refer to the chart illustrating these patterns of communication during this explanation.

4. Remind the parents that they can divert discipline problems from happening by observing and interpreting the signs of anger and frustration in their child. By using good conversation and listening skills, they can help put an end to discipline problems.

5. Inform them that their child has experienced this activity at school and that they can practice this skill at home.

6. Remind parents that by practicing good listening, conversation, and observation skills at home with their child, they are reinforcing the need to practice these skills at school. Through this collaborative effort they can prepare their child to avoid discipline problems with classmates at school.

Procedure (30 minutes)

The leader will conduct this activity as follows:

1. Seat the parents in a full circle.

2. Ask for a volunteer to act as a recorder.

3. Ask the parents to brainstorm typical examples of verbal and nonverbal patterns of communication that family members practice at home.

4. Ask the recorder to record these items on the paper pad.

5. After they have arrived at a list of items, ask them to discuss and arrive at a consensus as to which items are the most obnoxious.

6. Ask the parents to explain why an item offends them the most.

7. Continue this discussion by asking the following questions:

   • When your son or daughter gets home from school, how can you tell what kind of day he/she has had?

   • Describe the kind of verbal and nonverbal communication that your son or daughter exhibits.

   • How do you react to this behavior?

Appreciation (omit)

Instructional Tips

1. If there is a large number of parents (30 or more), divide them into two groups. Ask an associate to assist you with this activity.

2. Refer to examples of verbal and nonverbal patterns of communication in Section II, activity 5.

Anticipated Results

✓ The parents understand how to observe and interpret the meaning of verbal and nonverbal patterns of communication. They feel competent in interpreting the feelings behind specific messages.

✓ They understand how to observe and interpret signs of anger and frustration to prevent discipline problems from erupting between them and their child.

SESSION IV—ACTIVITY 9

LEARNING HOW TO EMPATHIZE WITH OTHERS

Purpose

To understand how to listen from your heart so that you can get in touch with another person's feelings.

Skill Development

The parents will learn how to:

✓ understand the feelings behind the words and actions of another person

✓ employ reflective listening techniques to convey an understanding of a person's message

Materials

• Reflective Listening Techniques handout (from Section II, activity 6)

• Words Illustrating Feelings and Emotions handout (from Section II, activity 6)

Introduction (5 minutes)

The leader will introduce this activity as follows:

1. Tell the parents that tonight they will learn to listen from their heart to get in touch with their children's feelings.

2. Explain that when hearing what their children are saying, they must understand the feelings behind the words and actions of their son or daughter. They must "put themselves in the shoes" of their children and try to experience what they are feeling.

3. Explain that to empathize with their children, they must put aside their own concerns and become more interested in their children than in themselves. This is done through reflective listening techniques that show their children they care about their feelings and understand the content of their message.

4. Inform the parents that through reflective listening techniques, they can prevent discipline problems from happening between them and their child because of a misunderstanding in the interpretation of a message.

5. Remind them that their child has experienced this activity at school and they should practice reflective listening techniques to:

   • quell discipline problems at home

   • prepare their child to divert discipline problems from developing at school

6. Refer to the handout describing the reflective listening techniques during this introduction.

Procedure (30 minutes)

The leader will conduct this activity as follows:

1. Seat the parents in a circle.

2. Pass out and review the Reflective Listening Techniques handout.

3. Refer them back to their list of items in activity 8.

4. Ask for a parent to volunteer to do a role-practicing activity with you.

5. Ask the parent to select a verbal or nonverbal style of communication that he/she disliked the most from the list of items.

6. To begin the role practicing activity, ask the parent an open-ended question, such as: "Why does this (name the style of communication) offend you the most?

7. Use reflective listening techniques to convey that you are in touch with his/her feelings, and that you understand his/her message.

8. After two minutes of conversation, ask the observing parents to identify and describe the reflective listening techniques used by the leader.

9. Next, ask the parents to role practice the same activity with another parent.

10. After two minutes ask the parents to switch roles.

11. Move around the room and assist as needed.

Discussion (10 minutes)

Lead a discussion by asking the following questions.

- Which reflective listening techniques did your partner use?
- How did your partner show that he/she cared for your feelings?
- What did you learn from this activity?

Appreciation (5 minutes)

Ask each parent to say one positive thing about what their partner did or said during tonight's activity.

Instructional Tips

1. Remind the parents that activity 8 complements activity 9. They initially learned how to observe and interpret a person's feelings, so they can then convey an understanding of their feelings through reflective listening techniques.

2. Refer to Instructional Tips, a list of reflective listening techniques and a list of feeling words, in Section II, activity 6.

Anticipated Results

✓ The parents understand how to get in touch with feelings that represent the words and actions of others. They are competent in conveying this message through reflective listening techniques.

✓ They understand how the use of reflective listening techniques to empathize with their child can prevent discipline problems from evolving at home.

SESSION V—ACTIVITY 10

LEARNING HOW TO MAKE I-FEEL STATEMENTS

Purpose

To understand how to replace negative "you" statements with positive "I-Feel" statements.

Skill Development

The parents will learn how to:

✓ make and use I-Feel statements

✓ communicate feelings by arriving at "I-Feel" messages to replace negative "you" messages

Materials

- "I" and "You" Messages Worksheets (from Section II, activity 8)
- "I" and "You" Messages handout (from Section II, activity 8)
- List of feeling words (from Section V, activity 9)

Introduction (5 minutes)

The leader will introduce this activity as follows:

1. Explain that the purpose of tonight's activity is for them to learn how to communicate through I-Feel statements.

2. Remind the parents that they are responsible for their own feelings and the way they react to what friends or family members say or do to them.

3. Tell the parents that they need to let family members or friends know how their behavior affects them.

4. Explain that it is easy to say the wrong thing and put the other person down or offend the other person via a "you" statement (refer to the list of "you" statements). However, by learning to use I-Feel statements they will express their feelings in a direct way without offending others (refer to I-Feel statements).

5. Explain that most people use "you" messages which create friction among friends or family members. However, by using I-messages they can convey a message in a positive way without offending people they care about, including their children.

6. Remind parents that they can alienate their child by offending him/her through "you" messages. By saying positive I-statements, they can correct their child in a positive way without creating feelings of hostility.

7. Stress the fact that saying "you" messages to their child can cause anger, and discipline problems can result.

8. Inform the parents that their child has completed this activity at school. They should practice using I-messages at home to prevent discipline problems both at home and at school.

Procedure (30 minutes)

The leader will conduct this activity as follows.

1. Seat the parents around tables.

2. Pass out copies of the handout that illustrates the meaning of I-Feel and "you" messages to parents. Explain the three parts of an I-message and the differences of the two messages.

3. Pass out "I" and "You" Messages Worksheet and list of feeling words to all parents.

4. Explain how to construct I-messages and "you" messages by completing the worksheets. Do this by reviewing situation 1 on the worksheet and by reviewing how to select the appropriate feeling words from the list.

5. Ask the parents to work in pairs or individually if they prefer.

Discussion (omit)

Appreciation (omit)

Instructional Tips

Refer to Instructional Tips, an explanation of "I" and "You" messages, a list of feeling words, and the "I" and "You" Messages Worksheet in Section II, activity 8.

Anticipated Results

✓ The parents understand how to arrive at I-Feel messages and the importance of replacing "you" messages with I-messages. They feel capable of arriving at and using an I-message in the appropriate context.

✓ They understand the importance of using I-messages to quell discipline problems from erupting between them and their child.

SESSION V—ACTIVITY 11

LEARNING HOW TO SAY I-FEEL STATEMENTS

Purpose

To understand how to use I-Feel messages in a direct and caring way.

Skill Development

The parents will learn how to:

✓ correctly use the three-part I-Feel statement

✓ be assertive and express true feelings in a direct and caring way

Materials

- List of Build-Up statements (from Section I, activity 6)
- "I" and "You" Messages handout (from Section II, activity 8)

Introduction (3 minutes)

The leader will introduce this activity as follows:

1. Explain to the parents that the purpose of this activity is to learn how to use I-Feel statements.
2. Remind them that learning how to make and use I-statements in the previous activity will help them to correctly use I-Feel statements.
3. Tell the parents that tonight they will use I-Feel statements to tell another person how they feel about how they are being treated. They will also say "you" messages to get a comparison of the two messages.
4. Remind the parents that they can use I-messages to discipline their child in a positive way.

Procedure (30 minutes)

The leader will conduct this activity as follows:

1. Ask the parents to meet in a full circle.
2. Pair off with a parent and role practice a situation.
3. Before beginning this activity, ask the parents to critique the role practicing demonstration. Review the illustrating "you" and "I-Feel" messages.
4. Begin by telling your partner where you plan to go on your vacation.
5. Ask your partner to interrupt you, give advice, or change the subject during this discussion.
6. Respond by illustrating an assertive "I-Feel" message and an aggressive "you" message.
7. After this demonstration, ask the observing parents to describe the difference between the use of an I-message and the use of a "you" message.

8. After the critique, ask the parents to pair off and practice the same activity.

9. After two minutes ask them to switch roles.

10. Move around the room and assist as necessary.

Discussion (10 minutes)

Lead a discussion by asking the following questions:

- What was difficult about using an I-Feel message?
- How can you simplify using an I-Feel message?
- How can you use an I-Feel message to improve how you communicate with a friend or family member?
- Do your friends or family members use "you" or I-messages? Describe.

  Pass out and review copies of the Build-up Statements to Parents

Appreciation (omit)

Instructional Tips

1. Refer to the same charts and illustrations that were used in activity 10.

2. Refer to instructional tips in Section II, activity 9.

3. Refer to Section I, activity 6, Building Self-Esteem Through Build-Up Statements. Show the parents examples of how to use build-up statements as opposed to putdown statements. Explain that they can use build-up statements along with I-messages to build the self-esteem of their children.

4. Pass out copies of a list of build-up statements and encourage the parents to use these positive statements to replace putdown statements. Refer to the list of build-up statements in Section I, activity 6.

Anticipated Results

✓ The parents understand how to use I-Feel messages in a direct and caring way; and they feel apt in using I-messages to express their true feelings.

✓ They understand the use of an I-message to discipline their child in a positive way.

DEFINING AND CLARIFYING
A PROBLEM

Purpose

To understand how to define and clarify a problem.

Skill Development

The parent will:

✓ learn how to define and clarify a problem

✓ practice using good open-ended questions and good listening skills

Materials

- Six-Step Critical-Thinking Process handout (from Section III, activity 1)
- Paper pads and marking pens

Introduction (3 minutes)

The leader will introduce this activity as follows:

1. Inform parents that tonight they will begin to learn critical thinking skills.
2. Pass out and review the Six-Step Critical-Thinking handout.
3. Explain that these skills will equip them to cope with or solve family problems.
4. Remind them that most teenagers have personal, family, school, and peer problems. Therefore, it is important for parents to have a process for helping their children cope with these problems.
5. Remind the parents that their child has practiced this activity at school and they can use this problem-solving process to help their child cope with a discipline problem at home or at school.

Procedure (30 minutes)

The leader will conduct this activity as follows:

1. Ask the parents to meet in a circle.

2. Lead a brainstorming session to arrive at typical discipline problems that teenagers have.

3. Ask for a volunteer to record these items on a paper pad.

4. After brainstorming for about 10 minutes, ask the parents to get a group consensus as to which problem area they would like to explore.

5. Assist the parents in arriving at their top choice.

6. Lead a discussion by asking the parents to share experiences they have had or have been exposed to within this problem area. Focus on discipline problems.

7. Ask open-ended questions and use reflective listening techniques to facilitate this discussion.

8. After each parent has told the group about his/her experiences, ask the parents to summarize the main ideas relative to their experiences, and to define and clarify their problem.

9. Ask the recorder to print these main ideas on a paper pad.

10. Summarize these ideas and arrive at a problem statement, and ask the recorder to print this statement on the paper pad.

Discussion (omit)

Appreciation (omit)

Instructional Tips

1. Refer to the steps for the critical thinking process in Section III, Introduction.

2. Refer to Section III, Activity 1, to review the Instructional Tips.

Anticipated Results

The parents understand how to define and clarify a problem area. They have successfully arrived at a typical discipline problem that affects their children on a personal level.

SESSION VI—ACTIVITY 13

ARRIVING AT AND EVALUATING
AN ALTERNATIVE SOLUTION

Purpose

To understand how to arrive at and evaluate alternative solutions that are necessary to solve a problem.

Skill Development

The parents will:

✓ learn how to arrive at and evaluate alternative solutions

✓ practice brainstorming, discussion, and positive communication skills

Materials

- Six-Step Critical-Thinking Process handout (from Section V, activity 12)
- Six-Step Problem Solving handout (from Section III, activity 1)
- Steps for Implementing a Decision handout (from Section III, activity 2)
- Paper pad and marking pen

Introduction (5 minutes)

The leader will introduce this activity as follows:

1. Explain to the parents that tonight they will cover steps 2 and 3 of the problem-solving process to:
   - arrive at alternative solutions for solving the problem
   - evaluate each of these solutions to arrive at the best solution for solving the problem
2. Remind the parents that they are practicing steps 2 and 3 in preparation for solving a discipline problem at home between themselves and their child. To facilitate this activity, their child has experienced this activity at school.
3. Remind the parents that by working with the teacher, counselor, and their child to solve discipline problems at home and at school, they are an important "link" in the Collaborative Discipline program.

4. Refer to the handout illustrating the six-step process and interpret the meaning of steps 2 and 3.

Procedure (30 minutes)

The leader will conduct this activity as follows:

1. Seat the parents in a circle, and pass out copies of the problem solving handouts.

2. Refer the parents to their problem statement from activity 12, and give them an opportunity to ask questions or add information to further clarify the problem area.

3. Monitor this discussion for five minutes, and rewrite the problem statement if necessary.

4. After the final problem statement has been agreed upon, ask the parents to print this statement on step 1 of their Six-Step Problem Solving handouts.

5. Lead a brainstorming session to arrive at alternative solutions to solve the problem.

6. Ask for a recorder to record these solutions on the paper pad, and remind the parents to copy these solutions on step 2 of their problem-solving handout.

7. Move to step 3 to review the pros and cons of each alternative solution.

8. Ask the parents to arrive at a positive and a negative consequence for each alternative solution and copy these consequences under the Positive and Negative headings on their problem solving handouts.

9. Ask the recorder to copy the pros and cons on the paper pad as the parents arrive at the positive and negative consequences of each alternative solution.

10. Remind the parents to copy this information from the paper pad on to step 3 of their problem solving forms.

Discussion (omit)

Appreciation (omit)

Instructional Tips

1. Remember to divide the parents into two groups when you have large numbers. Through this approach, parents will have a better opportunity to get involved or participate in the activity. Again, ask an associate to assist you in this instance.

2. Refer to the Instructional Tips in Section III, activity 2 and the problem solving and decision-making forms.

Anticipated Results

✓ The parents understand how to arrive at and evaluate alternative solutions. They have successfully arrived at the pros and cons of each solution for solving the problem.

✓ They understand how to use this process to solve a discipline problem between themselves and their child.

SESSION VI—ACTIVITY 14

MAKING AND IMPLEMENTING A DECISION

Purpose

To understand how to make and implement a decision.

Skill Development

The parents will:

✓ learn how to make and implement a decision

✓ practice discussion and good communication skills

Materials

• Six-Step Critical-Thinking Process handout (from Section V, activity 13)

• Paper pad and marking pen

• Problem-solving and decision-making handouts (from Section V, activity 13)

Introduction (2 minutes)

The leader will introduce this activity as follows:

1. Explain to the parents that tonight they will decide upon the best alternative solution, and they will learn how to implement their decision.

2. Tell them they will cover steps 4, 5, and 6 of the problem-solving process (refer to the outline and review these steps).

3. Remind the parents that their child has experienced steps 4, 5, and 6, and he/she is equipped to practice this process with them to solve a discipline problem at home.

4. Remind the parents that when their child practices the problem solving steps at home, their child is gaining additional experience to enhance her/his ability to cope with discipline problems in the classroom.

Procedure (30 minutes)

The leader will conduct this activity as follows.

1. Ask the parents to bring their problem solving and decision making handouts to this activity.

2. Seat the parents around tables.

3. Ask them to refer to the pros and cons on step 3 of their problem solving form.

4. Discuss the pros and cons with the parents, and ask them to think in terms of their own personal experiences as parents or other experiences related to their problem statement.

5. Tell them to focus on the negative and positive consequences of the pro and con items.

6. Through this discussion, ask the parents to arrive at a consensus as to which alternative solution or solutions are the best.

7. Ask the parents to record their decision on step 4 of their problem-solving form.

8. Move on to step 5 and ask the parents to copy their decision on step 1 of their Steps for Implementing a Decision Form.

9. Lead the parents through the decision making steps 2 to 5.

10. As the parents brainstorm items to complete these steps, the recorder will copy these items on the paper pad. The parents will record this information under the proper headings of their decision-making forms.

Discussion (omit)

Appreciation (omit)

Instructional Tips

1. Refer to Instructional Tips in Section III, activity 3, for additional information needed to conduct this activity.

2. If the parent group dwindles or begins to lose interest, provide time to discuss specific topics of interest related to parenting. Accordingly, the leader can table activity 14 and complete this activity at a later date. However, if the leader properly facilitates this activity, it should create a high level of interest.

Anticipated Results

✓ The parents understand how to make and implement a decision for solving a problem, and they have successfully designed an action plan giving them the steps needed to implement their decision.

✓ They understand how to use the problem solving process to solve a discipline problem at home between themselves and their child. They also understand that they are collaborating with the teacher, counselor, and the child to enhance the Collaborative Discipline Process to prevent discipline problems in the classroom.

SESSION VII—ACTIVITY 15

LEARNING IMPORTANT FACTS ABOUT TOBACCO, ALCOHOL, AND OTHER DRUGS

Purpose

To understand the harmful effects of tobacco, alcohol, and other drugs.

Skill Development

The parents will learn the facts and dangers of tobacco, alcohol, and other drugs.

Materials

- Paper pad and marking pen
- Current fact sheet listing facts about tobacco, alcohol, and other drugs.

Introduction (3 minutes)

The leader will introduce this activity as follows:

1. Explain to the parents that the purpose of tonight's session is to inform them about the harmful effects of tobacco, alcohol, and other drugs.

2. Inform the parents that tonight's session will be in two parts as follows:

- In part one they will discuss and list questions about what they would like to learn about substance abuse.

- In part two an expert will meet with them to answer their questions and provide them with the latest facts about drugs, alcohol abuse, and so on.

3. Inform parents that discipline problems involving their children can result at home and at school from drug abuse.

4. Remind them that if they are having discipline problems with their child because of drug abuse, they should ask the speaker about prevention programs that successfully treat teenagers with drug abuse problems.

Procedure (90 minutes)

The leader will conduct this activity as follows:

1. Seat the parents in a circle.

2. Lead a discussion about tobacco, alcohol, and other drugs by asking the following questions:

- How would you define the words tobacco, drugs, and alcohol?

- How do drugs and alcohol affect an individual?

- Which drugs are legal or illegal?

- Why do people use tobacco, alcohol, and other drugs?

- Are these substances easy to get?

- What are the dangers associated with these substances?

3. After 20 minutes of discussion, ask for a volunteer to tape five separate sheets of paper on the wall and record the headings: *alcohol, tobacco, marijuana, cocaine,* and other drugs such as *heroin, LSD.* or *PCP.*

4. Ask the parents to call out questions they have about a specific drug or drugs in general. Take one drug at a time and list the parents' questions.

5. Add questions of your own to the list.

6. Explain to the parents that sometimes we are reluctant to ask sensitive questions in public. Pass out 3 x 5 cards to record questions of a sensitive nature. Collect the cards and record the questions under the proper headings.

7. Introduce the speaker to the parents.

8. Ask the speaker to cover the latest facts and information about tobacco, alcohol, and other drugs.

9. After 30 minutes, facilitate a question-and-answer period that allows parents to ask their own questions or those resulting from the speaker's presentation.

Instructional Tips

1. It is recommended that the speaker be a physician with experience in the treatment and prevention of abuse of tobacco, alcohol, and other drugs.

2. In preparation for this activity, ask the speaker to inform the parents about the latest facts regarding tobacco, alcohol, and other drugs. In addition, they can offer interesting information relating to this subject, such as laws and the legality of drugs, treatment programs, prevention programs, latest trends on:

   - children taking drugs
   - gangs, violence, and drugs
   - effects of drugs on pregnant women
   - babies born as addicts

3. The teacher and/or speaker should pass out fact sheets or other pertinent information about tobacco, alcohol, and other drugs to the parents.

4. If time permits this activity can be divided into two parts. As described in the Introduction, Part 1 gives the parents additional time to prepare a list of questions for the speaker to answer. However, if time is a factor, omit Part 1 and the speaker can present a typical talk about tobacco, alcohol, and other drugs with a question-and-answer period.

Anticipated Results

✓ The parents have learned about the facts of drugs and alcohol and they understand the harmful effects of drugs and alcohol.

✓ They understand that discipline problems can result from drug abuse and they have become knowledgeable about prevention programs that treat teenage drug abuse.

TRANSITIONAL PLANNING

A goal of this collaborative discipline program is to:

✓ prevent at-risk students from misbehavior that results in discipline problems in the classroom

✓ successfully help these students meet their annual long range educational goals

Students who have successfully completed Sections I, II, III, and IV of this guide will achieve the above goal. However, it is important to realize that these at-risk students are still in danger of "falling through the cracks" during the next school year. Consequently, transitional plans are designed to ensure that returning 10th and 11th grade students will not get into discipline problems at school.

It is recommended that the counselor, parents, and their child meet at the end of the school year to make plans for the next school year. This course of planning should be done before the course of study is designed for each student for the coming school year. As a team, the counselor, parents, and child should decide upon a course of study and the classroom instructional program that best meets the needs of the student. For example, the following questions should be answered:

- Does the student need remedial instruction in mathematics, reading, or writing?

- Does the student need individualized instruction within a self-contained classroom?

- Does the student perform better within a cooperative study format?

- Will this student need a behavioral contract to prevent discipline problems in the classroom?

- Will this student need positive peer pressure from a student support team to deter him/her from getting into discipline problems?

- Is this student capable of succeeding academically through the regular school program?

- Is this student capable of mainstreaming into a regular classroom situation, such as a geometry or chemistry class?

- Should this student be involved in extracurricular activities or a part-time job during/after school hours to replace negative activities that contribute to discipline problems in the classroom?

Based upon a discussion of these questions, the above "team" collaborates to arrive at a transitional plan that will meet the educational and behavioral goals of the student. The following are examples of transitional plans of typical at-risk students:

Student Number One

Jane had always been a good student. However, during the first semester of the 11th grade she began having discipline problems in school—truancy and taking drugs with her friends. She failed some classes and lost some graduation credits. Jane's parents were concerned about her failing grades and met with Jane and her school counselor. During this counseling session, it was determined that Jane was making poor decisions in her choice of friends and the taking of drugs. She was easily led by negative peer pressure. Accordingly, they agreed to place Jane in an instructional program that focuses on student support activities. Through activity 10 in Section II of this book, she learned how to become assertive to resist negative peer pressure. And in Section III, activities 1, 2, and 3, she learned how to use critical-thinking skills to make good decisions and cope with a discipline problem. Through the positive support of her student teammates, teacher, counselor, and parents, Jane was able to make up the lost graduation credits during the second semester. Jane's parents attended the parent seminar activities. By learning good conversation and listening skills, they were able to discuss Jane's drug problem with her in an understanding and meaningful manner. They also used the six-step problem solving process to help her cope with her drug problem.

Through her career assessment and exploration program, Jane found that she is a data person. She is interested in and good at working with numbers. Her job choice is to become an accountant.

At the end of the school year, Jane met with her parents and the school counselor to design a transitional action plan for her senior year. (Refer to Jane's action plan following this section.)

Student Number Two

Jason is a member of a gang and has been caught bringing alcohol to school. He confronts authoritarian teachers who "lay down" the ground rules for class behavior, and he purposefully breaks rules to test the teacher. He also gets into conflicts with his peers through name calling, pushing, and an occasional fight. He is bigger and stronger than most boys his age, and he tends to be a bully. Consequently, Jason is constantly getting into discipline problems in the classroom.

Jason is a good student who is capable of making average and above average grades when he stays out of trouble and completes his course requirements. Because of Jason's gang involvement and his discipline problems in school, his parents are concerned that Jason might drop out of school. He has just completed 10th grade in high school. His parents want Jason to meet his full academic potential and graduate from high school. Accordingly, they met with Jason, a school counselor, and the teacher of a student support activities program.

Through this meeting, it was decided that Jason made some poor decisions in his choice of peer friendships and in the use of alcohol. His use of poor communication skills in relating to teachers and classmates has caused conflict between him and others. Because of these behavioral and communication problems, Jason has discipline problems in the classroom. Thus, the counselor, teacher, Jason, and his parents agreed that Jason could benefit from the student support activities program and he was enrolled in such a program. Through the student support activities, Jason was able to change his negative behavior to positive behavior. The "highlights" of these positive behavioral changes are as follows:

- Learning how to say build-up statements to replace put-down statements (Section I, activity 6)
- Learning how to monitor his own behavior and the behavior of teammates to become a team leader (Section 1, activity 10)
- Learning how to make and say I-Feel statements to replace "you" statements (Section II, activities 8 and 9)
- Learning how to become assertive to resist peer pressure (Section II, activity 10)
- Learning how to solve a discipline problem in the classroom (Section III, activities 1, 2, and 3)

Jason's parents met with the teacher, counselor and Jason to design a behavioral contract to be monitored in the classroom. They also attended the parent seminars. Consequently, Jason's parents learned the following communication and critical-thinking skills in preparation for helping Jason to meet the terms of his behavioral contract and succeed in school:

- Good conversation and listening skills (Section V, activities 5 and 6)
- How to observe others and empathize with others (Section V, activities 8 and 9)
- How to make and say I-Feel statements (Section V, activities 10 and 11)
- How to solve discipline problems (Section V, activities 12, 13, and 14)

Accordingly, Jason's parents collaborated, through the Collaborative Discipline Program, with the teacher, counselor, and Jason to help their son meet the terms of his behavioral contract and his educational goal of passing all subjects with a C or better letter grade average.

Through the career/leisure assessment program, Jason learned that he is a people person. He explored various jobs and leisure activities, discovering that he would like to be a youth counselor. He also renewed his interest in wrestling and boxing.

Jason successfully completed 11th grade and is anxious to finish 12th grade and graduate from high school. To ensure that Jason stays out of trouble and graduates from high school, Jason met with the school counselor and his parents to design a transitional action plan. (Refer to this plan following this section.)

Through this transitional planning procedure, the teacher, counselor, parents, and their child collaborate to prevent future discipline problems from occurring in the classroom. This planning enhances the Collaborative Discipline Program.

TRANSITIONAL ACTION PLAN

(Sample)

NAME _Jane_   DATE _June, 1994_

Educational Goal: _To graduate from high school_

Where will I go to reach my goal: _Central High School_

When will I begin my action plan: _September, 1994_

What steps will I take to reach my goal:

- _Enroll in a course of study to complete high school graduation requirements._
- _Enroll in a student support team cooperative learning instructional program._
- _Attend all classes on a regular basis, complete homework, and pass all tests._
- _Get a part-time job in a business or accounting office during/after school._

List barriers that might prevent me from reaching my goal:

- _Making contact with past friends and taking drugs._
- _Being truant from school._
- _Not completing homework assignments and failing course examinations._
-

Ways to deal with barriers:

- _Get support from student support team and make new friends._
- _Get part-time job to occupy time during after-school hours._
- _Plan a study schedule to complete homework assignments in the evening._
-

Deadline for initiating my action plan: _September, 1994_

TRANSITIONAL ACTION PLAN

(Sample)

NAME Jason   DATE June, 1994

Educational Goal: To graduate from high school

Where will I go to reach my goal: Central High School

When will I begin my action plan: September, 1994

What steps will I take to reach my goal:

- Enroll in college preparatory classes.
- Attend classes on a regular basis.
- Complete homework assignments and pass all tests with B and A letter grades.
- During after-school hours participate on the school wrestling team and after wrestling season get a part-time job as a youth leader for the City Recreation Dept.

List barriers that might prevent me from reaching my goal:

- Making contact with past gang members and becoming truant.
- Drinking alcohol with gang members.
- Staying out late at night with girlfriend and not completing homework.
-

Ways to deal with barriers:

- Plan a study schedule and complete homework assignments.
- Get involved in after school-wrestling and work as a youth leader.
- Thus, I'll replace negative activities with productive after-school activities.
- Strive to reach my goal of graduating from high school.

Deadline for initiating my action plan: September, 1994

TRANSITIONAL ACTION PLAN

NAME _____ DATE _____

Educational Goal: _____
_____

Where will I go to reach my goal: _____

When will I begin my action plan: _____

What steps will I take to reach my goal:

- _____
- _____
- _____
- _____
- _____

List barriers that might prevent me from reaching my goal:

- _____
- _____
- _____
- _____
- _____

Ways to deal with barriers:

- _____
- _____
- _____
- _____

Deadline for initiating my action plan: _____

REFERENCES

Albert, Linda, Roy, Will and LePage, Andy (1989). *Cooperative Discipline: How to Manage Your Classroom and Promote Self-Esteem,* American Guidance Service, Circle Pines, Minnesota, 55014–1796, Library of Congress Catalog Card Number:89–85059, ISBN–0–88671–362–5.

Byers, George H., North, Larry, Wolhner, Lou (1985). *Career Development: An Independent Study Course,* Santa Clara County Office of Education, 100 Skyport Dr., MC 236, San Jose, California, 95115, 408–453–6624.

Carroll, Susan (1985). *Skills for Adolescence,* the Quest National Center, 6655 Sharon Woods Blvd., Columbus, Ohio, 43229, 614–882–6400. (This curriculum guide is available only with the specialized teacher preparation that accompanies it.)

Daane, Calvin (1982). *Vocational Exploration Group,* Studies for Urban Man Inc., P.O. Box 1039, Tempe, Arizona, 85281, 602–946–6190

Daane, Calvin (1982). *Work & Leisure Satisfactions,* Studies for Urban Man Inc., P.O. Box 1039, Tempe, Arizona, 85281, 602–946–6190.

Davis, Helena (1986). *The Community Boards Program, Inc.: Starting a Conflict Managers Program,* Community Board Center for Policy and Training, 149 Ninth St., San Francisco, California 94103.

Gibbs, Jeanne (1987). *TRIBES: A Process for Social Development and Cooperative Learning,* Center Source Publications, 1207 Fourth St., P.O. Box 436, Santa Rosa, California, 95402.

Hartzler, Lynn P., and California Consortium for Independent Study (1989). *Revised Independent Study Operations Manual,* California State Department of Education, Sacramento, California 94244–2720 (721 Capitol Mall, P.O. Box 944272), 916–322–1048.

Michels, Bob, and Central Independent Study Staff (1990). *Central Independent High School Operations Manual,* 1800–C Fruitdale Ave., San Jose, California 95128.

Morlan, John E. (1974). *Classroom Learning Center: Planning, Organization, Materials, and Activities,* Fearon Pitman Publishers, Inc., 6 Davis Dr., Belmont, California 94002, Library of Congress Catalog Card Number: 73–77592, ISBN 0–8224–1410–4.

Nemko, Barbra (1986). *Model General Occupational Employability Skills,* University of California, Davis, Department of Applied Behavioral Sciences, Davis, California 95616

Rhodes, Donna C. (1986). *A Blueprint for Success: Collaboration with National Organizations for Dropout Prevention,* National Foundation for the Improvement of Education, 1201 Sixteenth St., N.W. Washington, DC 20036, (202) 822–7840.

Rohnke, Karl (1984). *Silver Bullets: A Guide to Initiative Problems, Adventure Games and Trust Activities,* Project Adventure, PO Box 100, Hamilton, Massachusetts 01936, (508) 468–7981.

Schoel, Jim, Prouty, Dick, and Radeliffe, Paul (1988). *Islands of Healing: A Guide to Adventure Based Counseling,* Project Adventure, Inc., P.O. Box 100, Hamilton, Massachusetts 01936, (617) 468–7981.

Slavin, Robert (1986). *Using Student Team Learning: The Johns Hopkins Team Learning Project,* Center for Research on Elementary and Middle Schools, Johns Hopkins University, 3505 North Charles St., Baltimore, Maryland, 21218, 301–338–8249.

Smuin, Stephen K. (1978). *Turn-Ons: 185 Strategies for the Secondary Classroom.* Fearon Pitman Publishers, Inc., 6 Davis Drive, Belmont, California 94002, Library of Congress Catalog Number: 77–929031. ISBN–0–8224–7051–9.

Varenhorst, Barbara B. (1980). *Curriculum Guide for Student Peer Counseling Training,* Varenhorst, 350 Grove Drive, Portola Valley, California 94025, 415–851–8001.

Youth at Risk Coordination Committee (1987). *Factors Related to Youth-at-Risk,* Santa Clara County Office of Education, 100 Skyport Dr., San Jose, California 95115, 408–453–6629.

RESOURCES

Basic Skill Assessment

Jastak, Associates Inc., P.O. Box 4460, Wilmington, DE 19807, (800) 221–WRAT, Wide Range Achievement Test. (Test is used to determine Reading, Spelling, and Mathematics grade level scores.)

Basic Skills Inventory, Los Angeles County Office of Education, Division of Juvenile Court Schools, 9300 E. Imperial Hwy., Downey, California 90242–2890.

Test was developed by Los Angeles County Office of Education, Attendance, and Pupil Services, Copyright 1985 by Los Angeles County Office of Education. A contact person is Darwin Lumley, principal of Los Padrinor Juvenile Hall, 7285 E. Quill Dr., Downey, California 90242, 213–803–6648. (Inventory diagnoses basic skills competency needs in Reading, Mathematics, and Language Arts.)

Vocational Assessment

Edits, P.O. Box 7234, San Diego, California 92107, Assessment includes COPS (career interest survey), COPES (career work values survey), and CAPS (career abilities survey), and a Comprehensive Career Guide that provides a profile summary that matches a student's career interests, values, and abilities with the appropriate career field.

Occupation Handbook, Bureau of Labor Statistics, Sales Publications Center, P.O. Box 2145, Chicago, Illinois 60690. (Handbook includes over 225 [updated] occupations.)

Learning Style Surveys

Burgess, Robert, Coordinator Student Services and School Climate, Almeda County Office of Education, 313 West Winton Ave., Hayward, California 94544–1198, 415–887–0152 Ext. 346 (Learning style inventory is used to determine visual, auditory, and kinesthetic [hands-on] learning styles.)

Reckinger, Nancy, Ed.D., *Personality Style Identifier: How to Use It, and Descriptions of Learning, Teaching, and Parenting Styles,* California State University, Fullerton, California 92634, 714–773–3411.

Seymour, Norma Jean, Ph.D., *Elementary and Secondary Suggested Remediation Strategies Which Capitalize on the Learning Style Strength,* 714–551–1590, 714–999–3535 P.O. Box 17784, Irvine, California 92713. (*Note*: Dr. Seymour has designed a Learning Style Inventory.)

Specific Language Disability

The Charles Armstrong School, 1405 Solano Dr., Belmont, California 94002, 415–592–7570. This school uses the Slingerland Multisensory Approach for children with Specific Language Disability. Visitations can be arranged and specialized training is offered during the summer months to learn this style of teaching.

Irlen Institute, 4425 Atlantic Ave., Suite A–14, Long Beach, California 90807, 213–422–2723. Contact person is Helen L. Irlen. This institute diagnoses visual perception problems and then prescribes appropriate color-tinted paper to type assignments on.

Community-Based Learning

City-As-School, Joyce Lazzeri, 1575 Old Bayshore Hwy., Burlingame, California 94010, 415–692–4300. This program is designed to link students to a variety of learning experiences throughout the community, to gain experience-based learning in business, civic, cultural, and other professional organizations.

Experience-Based Career Education, Far West Labs, Robert Schume, Field Studies Development, UCLA, 405 Hilgard Ave., Los Angeles, California 90025–1514, 213–825–7867. This program designs learning projects for students to experience in the community with business professionals, to meet their career and educational interests and abilities.

Exemplary Alternative School Programs

The Foundry School, Santa Clara County Office of Education, Alternative School Department, John Malloy (counselor), 258 Sunol St., San Jose, California 95126, 408–294–3838. This school program has a strong behavioral component that features counseling and participation in group dynamics and self-realization activities. Visitations can be arranged to view this program.

Peninsula School, Peninsula Way, Menlo Park, California 94025, 415–325–1584. This program features hands-on experience-based learning and is an excellent model for teaching the kinesthetic or hands-on action-oriented learning style. Visitations can be arranged to view this program.

Adventure Trust-Building Activity

ROPES, Conti, Dee, Central Independent High School, 1800–C Fruitdale Ave., San Jose, California, 95128. This activity puts students through a ROPES course that includes trust-building activities as students spot and support each other (as a team), while going through a series of physical exercises.

ROPES, Project Adventure, Inc., Box 100, Hamilton, Massachusetts 01936, 617–468–7981. To obtain information about tools and materials necessary to build a ROPES course obtain Challenge ROPES Course Source Book from Project Adventure, or to have a ROPES course constructed for you contact Project Adventure and they will send a staff of trained personnel to design/construct a ROPES course that is appropriate for your needs and budget. A ROPES course includes a series of obstacles made of ropes and cable, designed to promote team cooperation and individual achievement. These structures are built outdoors in tree settings or with telephone poles, or indoors using existing wall or beams for attachment points of elements.

INDEX

INTRODUCTION

This index matches specific activities to problem issues facing today's teachers and counselors. In order to provide immediate access to answers on solving specific problems, the index is organized as follows:

- Key words, such as *Conflict Resolution*, introduce each category.
- The section title, such as *Communication*, tells the teacher where the activities are located.
- The associated activities are listed under the section title.

For instance, a counselor can look up *Conflict Resolution* and select a number of activities that could curb or mediate a situation. Then, if two students were in conflict, they could be asked to complete: Communication, activity 3, "Learning Good Listening Skills" together as a strategy to calm a dispute.

To properly use this index, teachers and counselors should identify key words that depict problem issues, and then refer to specific activities as a means for dealing with these problems.